THE CREATIVE SOCIETY

We stand here on the only island of freedom that is left in the whole world. There is no place to flee to . . . no place to escape to. We defend freedom here or it is gone. There is no place for us to run, only to make a stand. And if we fail, I think we face telling our children, and our children's children what it was we found more precious than freedom.

Ronald Reagan

THE CREATIVE SOCIETY

Some Comments on Problems
Facing America

by

Ronald Reagan

THE DEVIN-ADAIR COMPANY
NEW YORK   1968

WHAT MANNER OF MAN?

ONE would have to search far to find another State Governor
who has taken as vital an interest in non-political topics . . .
the topics that mark the statesman rather than the politician
. . . as has Ronald Reagan of California.

Tom Wicker of the *New York Times* says that Reagan's
"greatest asset is that he is not trying to fool anybody; he is
simply saying what he thinks." And what Ronald Reagan
thinks is very much to the point in an era of confusion,
double-talk and fear. Here is the Reagan mind at work,
reaching its own conclusions after doing its own thinking.
The speeches that have drawn crowds and made headlines
are almost entirely self-written, a fact that sets him far apart
from the average office-holder we Americans have endured
in recent years, men whose pandering for votes has brought
us to a new low in our political history.

Ronald Reagan has had a wide experience in business,
labor, the theater and politics. Because of this and because
of a most appealing personality he has emerged as a man of
destiny, a bright new face in the Republican party. Political
pundit Stewart Alsop has called him "the hottest new product on the Republican horizon."

The pages that follow, taken mostly from recent speeches,
will answer the questions currently on many minds:

What *about* Ronald Reagan?

Is he just another politician?

Is he qualified to hold the highest office in the land?

Reporters, TV interviewers and political analysts have all tried to assess this dynamic Governor of California. *Saturday Review* noted that "wherever he went he probed for issues that were disturbing the voters." The article also noted that Reagan's "highly advertised charisma is creeping across state borders." *Newsweek* magazine observed that even his newness to public office could be "a virtue, crystallizing spreading public distaste for professional politicians . . ."

Asked by *Time* magazine to explain his changeover from liberal, New Deal Democrat to Republican, Reagan put it this way:

"You have to start with the small-town beginnings. You're a part of everything that goes on. In high school I was on the football team and I was in class plays and I was president of the student body, and the same thing happened in college. In a small town you can't sit on the sidelines and let somebody else do what needs doing; you can't coast along on someone else's opinions. That, really, is how I became an activist. I felt I had to take a stand on all the controversial issues of the day; there was a sense of urgency about getting involved."

Eventually his disillusion with the liberals became complete:

"I have come to realize that a great many so-called liberals aren't liberals—they will defend to the death your right to agree with them."

A glance at the table of contents of this book will indicate the wide-ranging issues that Ronald Reagan has tackled, and his own words prove what a California GOP Chairman said:

"He's a self-directed, self-motivated man. Nobody can force him to do things."

"The most magnetic crowd-puller California has seen since John F. Kennedy stumped the state in 1960," *Time* magazine observes. Political writer M. Stanton Evans adds to that comment that there is one difference between the two: "Kennedy lost California by 35,000 votes; Reagan carried it by nearly a million."

The *New York Times* tried to figure out why Reagan's popularity seems to go up no matter how strenuous the controversies in which he is involved. The *Times* concluded that the experts "just don't realize that you can't judge Reagan by the old standards. He makes them obsolete."

"Reagan is undisputably a part of America," concludes *National Review*, "and he may become a part of American History."

The Publisher

NOTE: *This book may be purchased in quantity from the publisher at the following prices:*

1-9	copies	$2.00	each
10-49	"	1.50	"
50-99	"	1.25	"
100-999	"	1.00	"
1000 or more	"	.85	"

order from
The Devin-Adair Company
23 East 26 St.
New York, 10010

CONTENTS

1. THE CREATIVE SOCIETY

FREEDOM is a fragile thing and is never more than one generation away from extinction. It is not ours by inheritance;
it must be fought for and defended constantly by each generation for it comes only once to a people. Those who have
known freedom and then lost it have never known it again.

Knowing this, it is hard to explain those who even today
would question the people's capacity for self-rule. Will they
answer this: if no one among us is capable of governing himself, then who among us has the capacity to govern someone
else? Using the temporary authority granted by the people,
an increasing number lately have sought to control the means
of production as if this could be done without eventually controlling those who produce. Always this is explained as necessary to the people's welfare. But, "the deterioration of every
government begins with the decay of the principle upon
which it was founded." This is as true today as it was when it
was written in 1748.

Government is the people's business and every man, woman
and child becomes a shareholder with the first penny of tax

(From the Inaugural Message as Governor, Jan. 5, 1967.)

paid. With all the profound wording of the Constitution, probably the most meaningful words are the first three, "We, the People." Those of us who have been elected to Constitutional office or Legislative position are in that three-word phrase. We are of the people, chosen by them to see that no permanent structure of government ever encroaches on freedom or assumes a power beyond that freely granted by the people. We stand between the tax-payer and the tax-spender.

It is inconceivable to me that anyone could accept this delegated authority without asking God's help. I pray that we who legislate and administer will be granted wisdom and strength beyond our own limited power; that with Divine guidance we can avoid easy expedients as we work to build a state where liberty under law and justice can triumph, where compassion can govern and wherein the people can participate and prosper because of their government and not in spite of it.

The path ahead is not an easy one. It demands much of those chosen to govern, but also from those who did the choosing. And let there be no mistake about this; we have come to a crossroad—a time of decision—and the path we follow turns away from any idea that government and those who serve it are omnipotent. It is a path impossible to follow unless we have faith in the collective wisdom and genius of the people. Along this path government will lead but not rule, listen but not lecture. It is the path of a Creative Society.

A number of problems were discussed during the campaign and I see no reason to change the subject now. Campaign oratory on the issues of crime, pollution of air and water, conservation, welfare and expanded educational facilities does not mean the issues will go away because the campaign has ended. Problems remain to be solved and they challenge all of us. Government will lead, of course, but the answer must come from all of you.

We will make specific proposals and we will solicit other

ideas. In the area of crime, where we have double our proportionate share, we will propose legislation to give back to local communities the right to pass and enforce ordinances which will enable the police to more adequately protect these communities. Legislation already drafted will be submitted, calling upon the Legislature clearly to state in the future whether newly adopted laws are intended to pre-empt the right of local governments to legislate in the same field. Hopefully, this will free judges from having to guess the intent of those who passed the legislation in the first place.

At the same time, I pledge my support and fullest effort to a plan which will remove from politics, once and for all, the appointment of judges . . . not that I believe I'll be overburdened with making judicial appointments in the immediate future.

Just as we assume a responsibility to guard our young people up to a certain age from the possible harmful effects of alcohol and tobacco, so do I believe we have a right and a responsibility to protect them from the even more harmful effects of exposure to smut and pornography. We can and must frame legislation that will accomplish this purpose without endangering freedom of speech and the press.

When fiscally feasible, we hope to create a California crime technological foundation utilizing both public and private resources in a major effort to employ the most scientific techniques to control crime. At such a time, we should explore the idea of a state police academy to assure that police from even the smallest communities can have the most advanced training. We lead the nation in many things; we are going to stop leading it in crime. Californians should be able to walk our streets safely day or night. The law-abiding are entitled to at least as much protection as the law-breakers.

While on the subject of crime . . . those with a grievance can seek redress in the courts or Legislature, but not in the streets. Lawlessness by the mob, as with the individual, will not be tolerated. We will act firmly and quickly to put down riot or insurrection wherever and whenever the situation requires.

Welfare is another of our major problems. We are a humane and generous people and we accept without reservation our obligation to help the aged, disabled and those unfortunates who, through no fault of their own, must depend on their fellow men. But we are not going to perpetuate poverty by substituting a permanent dole for a pay check. There is no humanity or charity in destroying self-reliance, dignity and self-respect . . . the very substance of moral fibre. We seek reforms that will, wherever possible, change relief check to pay check.

How can it be that our affluent society, capable of producing goods and services in the amount of some eight hundred billion dollars a year, with an unfilled demand for skilled workers, at the same time can add tens of thousands of people each year to the welfare rolls, until the percentage who are living on public subsistence is greater than at any time in our history, even including the days of the Great Depression?

Well, we believe that it's possible, very possible, that the approach itself to welfare as we've known it in these recent decades could have something to do with this.

In the last ten years, while our state's population was increasing 39 percent, the cost of welfare in constant dollars in California went up 247 percent. As a state, we rank third in poverty and first, in the last few years, in the amount of federal poverty funds that are assigned there. Some of us out there think that welfare has at last revealed itself to be a colossal failure, just as charity is a failure unless it makes people independent of the need for it.

As presently constituted, welfare's great flaw and weakness is that it perpetuates poverty for the recipients of welfare, institutionalizes their poverty into a kind of permanent degradation. We think that it's time that we re-orient and re-direct welfare so as to stop destroying human beings and instead to start saving them.

We're trapped in a multiplicity of regulations and an administrative nightmare, imposed by federal regulations and red tape, that are an inseparable part of the federal grants and aid.

Fortunately, however, there are some loopholes. We discovered that we are permitted here and there to experiment, and so with the permission of the government in Washington, we've launched a pilot program in the area of welfare. We've taken all those multitudinous agencies that are dealing with this one particular problem and in one community, Fresno, we have put all of these programs into one. It is one coordinated effort under one director and we're going to feed the recipients of public subsistence into one end of this combined effort.

At a certain check-point, those who cannot provide for themselves, those who, whether it's through age or disability, must depend on the rest of us, will drop out of that program into this permanent subsidy on the public. We hope that in so doing and in streamlining this, we'll be able to prove that we can provide not only some of the necessities but some of the comforts that make life worth living for those unable to care for themselves.

It is ridiculous to find that there are eighteen separate categories of people on welfare. What does it matter why people are dependent if they are dependent? Our obligation is plain and simple: to provide for them, and we can do this by welfare in one considered effort.

But this is not the ultimate answer. Only private industry in the last analysis can provide jobs with a future. A great citizen of our state and a fine American, Mr. H. C. McClellan, has agreed to institute a statewide program patterned after the one he directed so successfully in the "curfew area" of Los Angeles. There, in the year-and-a-half since the tragic riots, fully half of the unemployed have been channeled into productive jobs in private industry and more than 2,600 businesses are involved. Mr. McClellan is serving without pay and the entire statewide program will be privately financed. While it will be directed at all who lack opportunity, it offers hope especially to those minorities who have a disproportionate share of poverty and unemployment.

In the whole area of welfare, everything will be done to reduce administrative overhead, cut red tape and return control as much as possible to the county level. And the goal will be investment in, and salvage of, human beings.

This administration will cooperate with the State Superintendent of Education in his expressed desires to return more control of curriculum and selection of textbooks to local school districts. We will support his efforts to make recruitment of out-of-state teachers less difficult.

On the subject of education . . . hundreds of thousands of young men and women will receive an education in our state colleges and universities. We are proud of our ability to provide this opportunity for our youth and we believe it is no denial of academic freedom to provide this education within a framework of reasonable rules and regulations. Nor is it a violation of individual rights to require obedience to these rules and regulations, or to insist that those unwilling to abide by them should get their education elsewhere.

It does not constitute political interference with intellectual freedom for the taxpaying citizens—who support the college and university systems—to ask that, in addition to teaching, they build character on accepted moral and ethical standards.

Just as a man is entitled to a voice in government, so he should certainly have that right in the very personal matter of earning a living. I have always supported the principle of the union shop even though that includes a certain amount of compulsion with regard to union membership. For that reason it seems to me that government must accept a responsibility for safeguarding each union member's democratic rights within his union. For that reason we will submit legislative proposals to guarantee each union member a secret ballot in his union on policy matters and the use of union dues.

A close liaison with our Congressional representatives in Washington, both Democratic and Republican, is needed so that we can help bring about beneficial changes in Social Security, secure less restrictive controls on federal grants and work for a tax retention plan that will keep some of our federal taxes here for our use with no strings attached. We should strive also to get tax credits for our people to help defray the cost of sending their children to college.

We will support a bi-partisan effort to lift the archaic 160-acre limitation imposed by the federal government on irrigated farms. Restrictive labor policies should never again be the cause of crops rotting in the fields for lack of harvesters.

Here in our own Capitol, we will seek solutions to the problems of unrealistic taxes which threaten economic ruin to our biggest industry. We will work with the farmer as we will with business, industry and labor to provide a better business climate so that they and we all may prosper.

This is only a partial accounting of our problems and our dreams for the future. California, with its climate, its resources and its wealth of young, aggressive, talented people, must never take second place. We can provide jobs for all our people who will work and we can have honest government at a price we can afford. Indeed, unless we accomplish this, our problems will go unsolved, our dreams unfulfilled and we will know the taste of ashes.

Californians are burdened with combined state and local taxes $113 per capita higher than the national average. Our property tax contributes to a slump in the real estate and building trades industries and makes it well nigh impossible for many citizens to continue owning their own homes.

For many years now, you and I have been shushed like children and told there are no simple answers to complex problems which are beyond our comprehension.

Well, the truth is, there are simple answers—there just are not easy ones. The time has come for us to decide whether collectively we can afford everything and anything we think of simply because we think of it. The time has come to run a check to see if all the services government provides were in answer to demands or were just goodies dreamed up for our supposed betterment. The time has come to match outgo to income, instead of always doing it the other way around.

The cost of California's government is too high; it adversely affects our business climate. We have had a phenomenal growth with hundreds of thousands of people joining us each year. Of course the overall cost of government must go up to provide necessary services for these newcomers, but growth should mean increased prosperity and thus a lightening of the load each individual must bear. If this isn't true, then you and I should be planning how we can put up a fence along the Colorado River and seal our borders.

Well, we aren't going to do that. We are going to squeeze and cut and trim until we reduce the cost of government. It won't be easy, nor will it be pleasant, and it will involve every department of government, starting with the Governor's office.

Let me reaffirm a promise made during the months of campaigning. I believe in your right to know all the facts concerning the people's business. Independent firms are making an audit of state finances. When it is completed, you will have that audit. You will have all the information you need to make the decisions which must be made. This is not just a problem for the administration; it is a problem for all of us to solve together. I know that you can face any prospect and do anything that has to be done as long as you know the truth of what you are up against.

We will put our fiscal house in order. And as we do, we will build those things we need to make our state a better place in which to live and we will enjoy them more, knowing we can afford them and that they are paid for.

I believe that all over America, there are citizens who believe government is their business. All they want is to be asked and to be told how they can be of help. Every problem that besets us, from drop-outs to disease, from job training to student loans, is being solved some place in this country right now by someone who did not wait for government.

Perhaps what we need is a system of inter-communication to learn and teach each other the solutions that have been found here and there to head off problems before they become a government project.

Now this does not mean there is no part for government to play. Government has a legitimate role, a most important role in taking the lead in mobilizing the full and voluntary resources of the people.

In California, we call this partnership between the people and government The Creative Society.

Some who are inclined to resent any dilutions of government's influence continue to charge that people like ourselves are turning back the clock.

The Creative Society is not a retreat into the past. It is taking the dream that gave birth to this nation, and updating it, and making it practical for the 20th century. It is a good dream. It is a dream that is worthy of your generation.

If, in glancing aloft, some of you were puzzled by the small size of our state flag . . . there is an explanation. That flag was carried into battle in Vietnam by young men of California. Many will not be coming home. One did, Sergeant Robert Howell, grievously wounded. He brought that flag back. I thought we would be proud to have it fly over the Capitol today. It might even serve to put our problems in better perspective. It might remind us of the need to give our sons and daughters a cause to believe in and banners to follow.

2. HAVE WE BEEN OUT OF TOUCH WITH REALITY?

EARLY in this decade, half-way around the world, a disciple of Gandhi's passive resistance—Pandit Nehru—lived in a world of collaboration—playing off east against west and believing he had the situation well in hand. In 1962 came a rude awakening when the Red Chinese poured across his border. Nehru promptly went into seclusion. Reuters of London—which has known every contact in Asia for decades—was two days in finding him. It asked for an evaluation of the situation. He gave Reuters just eight words: "We have been out of touch with reality."

Have we in the United States also been out of touch with reality?

Is this the message of last November 8th? Did a restless people—a vibrant people—express their discontent with the tired old clichés of the 30's? Did they tell us they were too self-reliant to sell their dreams of the future for the dull security of the ant heap?

(From a 1957 speech to the Republican State Central Committee, Milwaukee.)

A wind of change is blowing across our land. Democrats and independents alike are joining hands with us to protest at the polls what has been going on in their governments.

Last year:

They voted against going deeper and deeper into debt when we are supposed to be more prosperous than man has ever been.

They voted against a war on poverty which poverty is losing.

They voted against the idea that we can, as a state or nation, afford anything and everything simply because we think of it.

And because most people believe in reward for productive labor, they voted against giving that reward to those who are able to but unwilling to work.

They voted against the idea that government must grow ever larger, more costly, more powerful.

They voted against continuing an easy atmosphere of peace and prosperity while some young Americans are dying in defense of freedom.

We have reached a turning point in time. It is our destiny —the destiny of our party—to raise a banner for the people of all parties to follow; but choose the colors well, for the people are not in a mood to follow the sickly pastels of expediency—the cynical shades of those who buy the people's votes with the people's money.

Thousands upon thousands of Americans today are groping for answers to their doubts—seeking a cause in which they can invest their idealism and energy. And because there can be no vacuum in the area of human relations, some of them are finding the wrong cause.

Politics as usual would indicate that we should be taking positions not unappealing from any viewpoint. But statesmanship demands that we face reality with faith in the people's wisdom.

Half a million fighting men in Vietnam are dependent on

a lifeline of ships threading through the Russian-built mines
and torpedoes in the harbor of Saigon. Russian-built munitions to kill our fighting men enter the unmined harbor at
Haiphong to the north but we are told that if we do what the
enemy does and mine that harbor, the war will grow bigger
and more terrible.

In the meantime our leaders offer a trade deal to help increase Russia's industrial capacity. The press reports that our
government had in mind the purchase of giant generators
from Russia for our own Grand Coulee Dam—while we
worry about our unemployed.

It would be the height of folly for us to attack the
patriotism and the sincerity of those who believe that the
enemy's hostility and announced intention to destroy our
way of life will turn to friendship if, regardless of provoca-
tion, we add to his strength.

But we can challenge their naïveté and their lack of touch
with reality.

Within a one-week period we have seen a war in the Mid-
East begin, and end, and it did not bring on World War III.
A small nation, faced with the denial of its sovereignty—
indeed, of its very existence—reminded us that the price of
freedom is high but never so costly as the loss of freedom.

Once again, when the sound of battle came, men in high
places in our government were caught by surprise. Having
backed away from those decisions they should have made
earlier, they are faced with drastic and extreme alternatives.

Those who have followed our banner—the Republican
banner—want to know and should know our stand on those
issues and problems that plague our nation. Because freedom
is indivisible, we must make it clear that we oppose all those
who deny freedom to anyone in our land because of race, religion or national origin.

We must guarantee every citizen his right to share in an
abundant society proportionate to his ability. But we will not
tolerate those who use either "civil rights" or the "right of

dissent" as an excuse to take to the streets for riot and mob violence—under the euphemism of civil disobedience.

Let our banner also proclaim that we will accept responsibility for eliminating the poverty of the genuinely poor, but that we shall deny the arrogant misuse of poverty funds for political nest-building.

Here, in the richest nation in the world where more crime is committed than in any other nation, we are told that the answer to this problem is to reduce our poverty. Well, this is a worthy goal in itself, but it isn't the answer. During the dark days of the depression, when poverty was rampant, the crime rate was at an all time low.

Government's function is to protect society from criminals, and not the other way around. The criminal is responsible for his misdeeds, not society. His punishment must be swift and certain. Trials are held to determine guilt or innocence. They are not exercises in the use of legal technicalities.

In short, our banner must be a symbol of our belief that government exists for the convenience of the people—that our national purpose is to provide the ultimate in individual freedom, consistent with law and order.

And if this is the banner you would raise, then you have come to the moment of truth.

3. GOVERNMENT NOT THE ANSWER

BACKWARD nations are backward and undeveloped nations are undeveloped not because of their climate and not because of their soil, but instead, for two other reasons:

—First, because of their political systems. Either they are too unstable as in many of today's so-called emerging nations or else these systems are in the grip of modern-day feudalism such as Russia's or China's.

—Second, because they lack both the know-how and the political structure necessary to build business, industry and commerce.

In the United States we have been blessed, not alone by our natural resources—other nations have great resources, too—but by our people, the world's most industrious, ingenious, enterprising and inventive, and by our political system—one of the few devised by man that is both stable and free. Stable enough to let a prosperous economy evolve and free enough to allow initiative and ingenuity to triumph over the dead hand of bureaucracy and regulation.

(*From an address before the Merchants and Manufacturers Assn., Los Angeles, and a speech at Anaheim at the Republican State Convention.*)

Now, before someone reads narrow chauvinism into this, let me assure you I'm well aware that the typical American is an immigrant or descendant of immigrants from any and every country of the world. The new dimension here that made his accomplishment possible was the subject of study by Herbert Hoover who declared the answer lay in one thing—"freedom." Here we unleashed the genius of every man by giving him freedom to an extent never known before by man anywhere.

Today, unfortunately, we see that freedom slowly vanishing on many fronts—all in the name of the common good—and stability sorely threatened by a political and social climate that acknowledges the rights of the individual, but not his responsibilities.

I know, those advocates of big government and more government controls point with pride to the state of our economy today. Well, I say that the economy is as good as it is today, not because of government rules and regulations and nitpicking, but in spite of it.

The best testimony to the vitality of American business and industry and the competence of the American businessman and industrialist is that they have managed to survive the rules and regulations with which they have been harassed for the last 35 years.

It makes one wonder how good business would be, just how much more industry and agriculture would be producing if they weren't hindered and hampered at every turn, if they weren't overburdened by regressive taxes, swamped with government-ordered paper work and threatened by thousands of rules and regulations promulgated by hundreds of unrelated, uncoordinated agencies at every level of government.

It makes one wonder how much better off we would be as individuals if government weren't prying and poking into every nook and corner of our daily lives. Actually, we need not wonder. There are answers if we pay them heed—for instance, that percentage of agriculture regimented for more than three decades has declined steadily in the per capita consumption of its produce while the larger unregimented percentage has increased per capita consumption of its produce 30 percent.

Take the war on poverty—a matchless boondoggle, full of sound and fury, but still with no record of accomplishment to point to. No one quarrels with the announced humanitarian goals, only with the abandonment of tried and true principles and the seeming belief that no answer is satisfactory unless it is a government answer.

The latest anti-poverty proposal is a multi-million dollar scheme to set up the Zuni Indians in a cooperative store to retail their handicraft jewelry. If it works (and the government says it will), they will gross $150,000 a year. Overlooked is the pertinent fact that the Zunis on their own already are doing $2 million a year in the sale of their jewelry.

With some understandable satisfaction, a month or two ago we vetoed a project in California to teach people how to picket and demonstrate.

Under the combat rules, I have the option of vetoing those various projects, although Washington has the right to overrule that veto within 30 days. Evidently, Washington hasn't had to override many vetoes because there haven't been many. We changed that situation when we vetoed a project in Ventura County that was aimed at rehabilitating the hardcore unemployed by putting them to work beautifying our open park lands. We didn't quarrel with the purpose, but when our research revealed there were 17 hard-core unemployed and half the money would go for seven administrators to take care of the 17 beneficiaries, we vetoed the project. The veto was not overridden.

All told, we have in these several months successfully vetoed seven projects and caused more than half of all the rest to be substantially changed before approving them.

Another program went into effect before our administration took office. This is the California Rural Legal Assistance Office with a budget of $1,545,874 and a total of 130 lawyers, investigators, secretaries and clerk-typists in 10 offices throughout California. This sounds just fine; legal help for the rural poor. But in at least one case, the California Rural Legal Assistance Office, using taxpayers' money, is harassing a county welfare office to the point where that county's Board of Supervisors has had to use the taxpayers' money to hire a lawyer at $35 an hour to protect its county welfare director. Her big problem was that she saved her county $200,000 in welfare costs last year. In the eyes of some of these people, saving taxpayers' money is a crime.

But this isn't the sole story of the California Rural Legal Assistance League. Many of their lawyers are actively and unethically promoting litigation, often against the state, once again leaving the taxpayer to pay both the costs of the prosecution and defense. Among the cases they have taken to court to the detriment of our state and our farmers is the suit to stop our changes in Medi-Cal, a suit, incidentally, which if they had won would have deprived 150,000 of our people of any kind of public medical care and would have cost one county alone, Los Angeles, an extra $20 million.

Another suit, if they had won it, would have cost California farmers millions in lost crops and the poor people other millions in higher food costs. That suit sought to prevent the importation of about 8,100 supplemental workers into California on an emergency basis. Incidentally, even labor Secretary Wirtz, no friend of California farmers, approved the effort to bring in workers. So we had a federal government body opposing an official of the President's cabinet.

The theory of Communism holds that government eventually will wither away. The theory of Socialism says that government is the answer to all the people's problems. The theory of the Creative Society says that government is best when kept closest to and most responsive to the people. That is the direction in which we are attempting to move. And that is why you have been hearing in recent months the outraged and anguished screams of those who do not trust the people to govern themselves.

Most of you know of our government-efficiency task force that is studying state government in order to make it more efficient, more economical and better able to cope with the people's needs. In fact, many of you and your firms have lent us some of the nearly 200 top-flight executives we have working on the project.

You would think—as I have thought—I guess we're all pretty naïve sometimes—that the willingness of business, of industry, of private citizens to volunteer their time and their money to help their state would win unanimous approval.

Instead, we have some disciples of "big government knows best" on our backs. They don't think private citizens should be messing around with their government. They don't think you and I have any real right to know what's going on there. They are suspicious of their fellow citizens who want to save the taxpayers' money instead of spending it. They cannot conceive of how an efficient goxernment could still be a government responsive to the people's needs.

Well, we have heard the criticism. And I can assure you that this non-partisan group—made up of both Republicans and Democrats—is going to continue with its task.

For two hundred years, American business and industry have fought the greatest war on poverty the world has ever known. At the height of the great depression they were employing ninety percent of the nation's workers.

There were proposals in those days, to help industry employ the other 10 percent. But the political climate shifted and we went instead to the hand-out, the dole and make-work projects, government-sponsored and government-run. And the only way we eliminated those, the only way we recovered under that approach was to become involved in a war. And the only way that approach still keeps the economy running high is by way of war, known today as "police action."

It should be obvious by now, although it doesn't seem to be in some quarters—that there must be another and better way. It should be obvious by now that a self-appointed group of experts operating out of either Washington or Sacramento cannot have all the answers to the problems that beset us.

And it should also be obvious that the sophisticated approach of seeking complicated answers by government to complicated problems isn't necessarily the best approach. Those of us who do not see a panacea in the approach of big brother and big government are often accused of over-simplifying, of not being aware of the complexities of modern-day life.

I reject that thesis. I say there are simple answers to many of our problems—simple but hard. One is that we, as a people, should turn to government only to help solve those problems we cannot solve ourselves. We turn to local government first, then to state government and only as a last resort to Washington.

These are answers that say the government hand-out and the government regulation are not the solution. These are answers that say the solutions to the people's problems lie with the people, that the people have genius and courage to solve their own problems. This is what I mean when I talk about the Creative Society.

Government must help, surely, government often must show the way and government may coordinate. But government must not supersede the will of the people or the responsibilities of the people. The function of government is not to confer happiness, but to give men the opportunity to work out happiness for themselves.

4. CRIME—1968

THE F.B.I. reports that the largest increase in serious crime in the last nine years took place in the first three months of 1967. Crimes of violence, murder, rape, robbery, assaults, were up 20 percent.

Since 1960 crime has increased by 35 percent, even when you allow for the increasing population. Crime is increasing four times as fast as our population. In fact, it has reached epidemic proportions. Imagine newspaper headlines announcing the threat of a nation-wide epidemic that would take nearly 10,000 lives, hospitalize another 200,000 and cause financial losses of more than a billion dollars.

The outcry would be tremendous. Yet, that is a description of our annual crime losses and the outcry has hardly risen above a whisper except in isolated instances.

We know that our biggest source of crime is our young male population—those between 14 and 29. In California, this group commits 80 percent of all crimes. And during

(From a speech to the National Sheriffs Assn., Las Vegas, and earlier remarks before the National Institute on Crime and Delinquency.)

the next 20 years this age group will increase twice as fast as the rest of our population. Needless to say, the effects could be devastating.

Already in our country few women are brave enough or foolhardly enough to venture out alone at night. Many neighborhoods are not even safe in the daytime.

There has been a significant increase in the purchase and training of watchdogs. More and more citizens are buying firearms, not for hunting or target practice, but for protection of themselves and their families.

Women are urged to carry whistles as a means of calling for help. Self-protection classes in judo and karate flourish. Law-abiding citizens are genuinely concerned. And so are those of us who are ultimately charged with providing protection, maintaining law and order, solving and preventing crime and finding causes of crime, and juvenile delinquency.

The threat to society by crime places a number of responsibilities on all of us at the state and local level who have a responsibility for the public safety.

First, we must focus public attention on this problem and enlist widespread public support in coping with it.

Second, we have a responsibility to make sure that the public receives the facts about the problem and about feasible solutions to it.

Third, we must make sure that we are making the best use of all available resources for preventing and controlling crimes.

Fourth, we must work to bring the best and the most modern scientific resources to bear on the crime problem.

Let me elaborate: effective law enforcement is primarily a local responsibility. Other levels of government, both state and federal, can supply assistance, but we must never forget that the basic tasks of crime prevention and control belong at the local level. This places a great responsibility on cities and counties to provide adequate support for their law enforcement officers, and to provide the necessary facilities and equipment for keeping the peace.

This is an area for partnership between state and local government, with local officials having the primary role and the state providing those services which must be statewide to be effective. It is important to recognize that unless both local and state law enforcement agencies meet their responsibilities, we may find them usurped by the federal government or ceded to it by default. When this happens we will have, in effect, a national police force. And we will have taken steps to abolish crime only at the risk of our freedom.

Another step in the war against crime must be the mobilization of public support. One of our aims has been to involve the citizen and the independent sector in government. There are many things government cannot do alone, and there are many things the independent sector can do better than government. You know, they may not believe it in Washington, but when given a chance, the average American wants to contribute to solving the problems which face us— including the crime problem.

In our state, we see citizens involved in crusades to "stamp out crime." We find businessmen forming parole advisory committees to aid our correctional program. We find industries interested in contributing funds and manpower to crime prevention programs. And this does make sense. When citizens and government work together to fight crime, it is the citizen who gains in terms of increased public protection.

There are not enough sheriffs and police to reverse the crime trend without the continuing support of our communities. Public information and community relation programs are no longer luxuries for law enforcement agencies. They must become essential parts of day-to-day operations.

A recent development shows that a cooperative partnership can exist between different levels of government. Our Highway Patrol has arranged a computer link-up between our

State Capitol and the National Crime Information Center at
F.B.I. headquarters in Washington. Twenty-nine police
agencies in California were linked on April 27, through the
California Highway Patrol computer, to the F.B.I. information system. We are told by J. Edgar Hoover that this is the
first computer-to-computer exchange in the history of law enforcement. In fact, it is the first use of this technological advance to link local, state and federal governments.

We feel it will be invaluable in our fight against crime by
allowing the rapid retrieval and exchange of information
between California and the F.B.I. and in this kind of legitimate cooperation there is no danger of local authority being
usurped.

But this is just one step. We are convinced that efforts now
being made throughout our state and nation must be better
coordinated, and that new efforts must be made if we are to
be truly effective in preventing and controlling crime.
Those engaged in this broad field must be able to share the
resources and the research, and benefit from the progressive
practices of others.

In order to achieve this, we are working with the state attorney general, leaders of local law enforcement, the judiciary, and the Legislature to develop a master plan for California criminal justice. We have four major objectives:

First, to provide for statewide planning and for orderly
and effective development in the field of criminal justice.

Second, we wish and expect to maintain the traditional
partnership and cooperation between the agencies of state
and local government.

Third, we must provide coordination of those agencies and
groups involved in criminal justice projects.

Fourth, we must provide a vehicle to handle federal-state
relations, and to implement federal legislation dealing with
crime control.

Under this plan, we hope to bring together all the agencies
and bodies involved in crime control, as well as representa-

tive citizens, to develop statewide plans for the prevention, detection and control of crime and for the improved administration of criminal justice. Such a plan will give California the ability to attack crime, and the roots of crime from many vantage points.

Of course, no program in itself can work miracles or eliminate crime, but we feel this program will insure that we are utilizing to the fullest all the available resources, and that we continually are searching for new resources in the never-ending war on crime.

But I think that just as important as the mechanical steps we are taking is a need to redirect the thinking of some of those engaged in the war on crime. I do not hold with the theory that says society is to blame when a man commits a robbery or a murder and therefore we must be understanding and as sympathetic for the criminal as we are for the victim. Nor do I hold with the spirit of permissiveness abroad in the land that has undoubtedly added to the juvenile delinquency problem.

This is an era, not only of permissiveness, but also of affluence. As a result many young people often have time on their hands. Many who might otherwise find jobs have no need to work. May I point out respectfully that we should question perhaps that part of the President's crime report that lays such emphasis on curing crime by eliminating poverty. This is a worthy goal in itself but it is interesting to note that during the great depression we had an all-time low in crime. Poverty is one contributing factor, but we should not delude ourselves that simply by improving social conditions we can automatically eliminate crime.

I cannot help but believe that goods and privileges carelessly given or lightly earned are lightly regarded. A boy who works for the money to buy a car and keep it in gasoline is much more likely to appreciate it and care for it than the youth whose car has been given to him and whose gas is purchased on his father's credit card. Likewise the boy or girl who can go out at night only if he or she behaves is more apt to behave than those who have no set rules to follow, and no responsibilities to accept.

This brings me down to two points. First, are we doing enough for our children by doing too much for them? Aren't they really better off if they are taught to accept responsibility and to learn that in the long run we all must earn what we get and that we usually get what we earn?

The second point is, haven't we made it almost impossible for many of our young people to earn legitimately the things they need and want?

In some cases we have taught them by example that they don't have to earn, that instead they have a right to expect to be given. I challenge that this is wrong. I challenge that nobody does any young person any favor by this approach.

But also, haven't our laws, aimed with the best intentions at preventing exploitation of children and providing old age security and of insuring meaningful wages—haven't these, by being too narrowly drawn and too rigidly implemented, put many kids to loitering on the street corners because they weren't allowed to get jobs after school or during the summer?

I suggest that if exceptions were made in some of our laws regarding social security and minimum wages, and if some of our unions would cooperate by recognizing that a boy seeking a part-time job should fall in a little different category than the full-time skilled or semi-skilled adult, that we would take a lot of our young people off the streets and out of trouble.

You know, there are a lot of old maxims that are still true today and it is not amiss to note that "it is idle hands that do the devil's work" and, as a result there is often the devil to pay and it is you and I who usually do the paying.

In urging that we allow our young people the right to work and to earn and to gain the sense of pride that you only get through your own accomplishments, I am not overlooking the value of recreation. I think, without question, that we need better and more recreational facilities. We need to make it possible for a boy or a girl to play hard as well as to work hard, and to develop and take pride in his athletic skills or hobbies.

I suggest to you that this is another area where government, with its limited tax funds, can turn to business and industry to sponsor teams, to make available recreational facilities and to work with youth on an informal basis. A slum boy living next door to a factory wouldn't be throwing rocks through the factory windows if the factory owners and foreman were friends who now and then extended a friendly hand. Here is an area in the independent sector that offers tremendous possibilities.

Now I do not mean by all this that there is no such thing as a bad boy or that there is no place in our society for punishment. Far from it. There is talk these days that punishment is not a deterrent, and I believe that talk is partly responsible for our increase in crime. As punishment becomes more difficult to mete out, those who would be deterred by its threat feel freer to resort to crime and acts of violence.

Some court decisions have narrowed the difference between liberty and license and in some areas have overbalanced the scales of justice so that the rights of society are outweighed by decisions granting new rights to individuals accused of crimes.

There was the case of the young boy who came home from school and found a man—a boarder in the home—washing blood from his hands in the kitchen sink. He told the boy he had cut himself.

The boy went into the bedroom where he found his 10-year-old sister's body hidden under clothing and papers.

He ran screaming from the house.

The little girl had been stabbed 60 times and had been mutilated in a savage and depraved manner. Cigarettes had been ground out in some of her wounds.

The murderer was convicted and sentenced to death. But the California Supreme Court in a 1-3 decision reversed the conviction and death penalty not because there was any question of his guilt but because of technical reasons and because "there was insufficient evidence that the defendant intended to commit mayhem or to torture."

Obviously, I'm not telling this with the idea of shocking you with a story of a crime of violence. I am telling it only to point up the need for common sense and realism in the war on crime. Let us have an end to the idea that society is responsible for each and every wrongdoer. We must return to a belief in every individual being responsible for his conduct and his misdeeds with punishment immediate and certain.

With all our science and sophistication, our culture and our pride in intellectual accomplishment, the jungle still is waiting to take over. The man with the badge holds it back.

As we look at the many problems facing law enforcement, we cannot afford to overlook the fact that mass criminal violations and mob violence are increasingly endangering our communities. Some euphemistically call this "civil disobedience." It is nothing more nor less than deliberate and premeditated violation of the law by groups of people. Protest that takes the form of criminal violations, leads to violence, mob rule, and ultimately to anarchy, where no man has either freedom or rights.

Those who go about the country forecasting "a long hot summer" and predicting where the next riots will take place contribute to disturbances and disorders because some of the more irresponsible elements seem to feel an obligation to justify these predictions.

I am also a little tired of those who proclaim that we must pour so much money into a community program, or enact this or that social legislation, *or else* we face a wave of riots and unrest. Government must be responsive to the needs of its citizens; it must provide equal opportunities in education

and employment; and it must work to alleviate adverse social conditions. But it must not bow to threats of violence
which amount to political extortion.

Most of the great increase in crime is accounted for among
those who have been born or reached maturity since World
War II. In California, as we have seen, 80 percent of all
crimes are committed by men and boys between 14 and 29.

The biggest increases in crime have been crimes against
property—burglary, auto theft and the like.

At the same time that crime has been rising, police ability
to meet the challenge posed by the criminal has diminished.
It has diminished to the point where it is difficult to say any
more that crime does not pay. Only about 25 percent of our
reported crimes are solved. I will leave it to you to decide
whether some court decisions rendered in recent years are at
least partly to blame for this shocking fact.

Even with only a 25 percent clearance rate, however, our
prisons which hold 27,000 are full and 14,000 more are on
parole. Our Youth and Adult Corrections Agency budget
costs California taxpayers 83 million dollars a year. The annual correctional bill nationally runs something over a billion dollars. And, of course, this is only a small fraction of the
total cost of crime prevention and control. If you add in the
cost of property losses, personal injuries and deaths, the total
reaches staggering proportions.

Obviously, something must be done to halt this trend. The
alternatives eventually are anarchy or a police state. Neither
is particularly inviting.

California, as I have said, is the leading state in terms of
major crimes. On a percentage basis, we have nearly twice our
share—nine percent of the population and about 17 percent
of the crime.

I am convinced that enactment of legislation we have introduced will help deter crime, will slow the flood of porno-
graphic material now available on our newsstands, will speed

and strengthen the administration of justice and will assure California citizens the best, most efficient law agencies in the nation.

This legislation includes:

—First: an effective law to restore to the cities and counties the ability to enact local laws designed to meet local problems. This is commonly referred to as the "implied pre-emption issue." Such a law will allow local law enforcement agencies to more thoroughly police their jurisdictions, especially in the areas of vice, sex offenses and offenses against public decency.

—Second: laws increasing penalties for those criminals who, during the commission of a robbery, burglary or rape, inflict great bodily harm upon their victims with dangerous weapons. I believe society must be protected from those who would inflict personal violence on its members. These bills, by the way, have already been passed and signed into law. We think they will be of major help in our war on crime.

—Third: comprehensive legislation dealing with pornography and obscenity, with special emphasis on prohibiting dissemination to minors of "harmful" material. A careful effort is being made to avoid any suspicion of censorship. Unfortunately, the legislation was recently held in committee on a straight party line vote even though it had the active support of our Democratic attorney general.

—Fourth: we recognize that from time to time persons are arrested unjustly or as victims of circumstances. Yet, despite their innocence, they must live the remainder of their lives with a public police record. Our bill, by closing certain records, will provide relief for such persons, while, at the same time, preserving those records for use by law enforcement and authorized persons.

But we are convinced that even more effort on the part of all of us is needed if we are to control crime.

A major reason, I think, for the increase in crime is the

very progress we are making which benefits and enriches our civilization.

Scientific and technological advances are being utilized by and adapted for use by the criminal element.

Modern methods of transportation and communications, and modern tools and weapons are used daily by those who prey on society.

If we are to reverse this trend, it is essential that society also use to the fullest our scientific and technological advances in the prevention, detection and control of crime. And in the correction and rehabilitation of criminals.

In addition, there is need for basic research involving the joint effort of various scientific and professional disciplines into the nature of crime, and crime apprehension and treatment.

We in this administration are also proposing that a California Crime Foundation be created as a public corporation. Such a foundation would be financed and served by both the private and public sectors. Its purpose will be to develop a coordinated state, local and private effort toward developing new scientific techniques to combat crime, initiate research projects in the area of police management, administration and basic research in the field of crime, and encourage engineers and scientists to devote themselves to careers in crime research.

We hope we can finance this foundation by channeling to it funds appropriated for some existing state law enforcement efforts and by winning the financial participation of private foundations and the business community. This is certainly one of those areas where the independent sector can be, and should want to be, of help.

Without respect for law, the best laws cannot be effective. Without respect for law enforcement, laws cannot be carried out. We must have respect, not only for the law, but also for the many who dedicate their lives to the protection of society through regular enforcement of the law.

5. THE RACE PROBLEM AND THE GHETTO

ONE problem in our nation overshadows all the others, and the cowardly hand of an assassin has laid that problem on America's doorstep.

Whatever your opinion of Martin Luther King, whether you approved or disapproved, our nation died a little when he died. It started dying and his murder began with our first acceptance of compromise with the law.

That compromise ranges from our indifference when some would apply the law unequally to some of our fellow citizens, to those who today, black or white, say it is up to us as individuals to decide which laws will be obeyed and which laws broken.

And it includes those in government, unless and until they have the courage to say the law will be enforced and will be enforced equally and applied to all men on an equal basis.

The time has come for all of us to make a choice. Either we reaffirm our faith in man's ability to meet his fellow man in a

(From a speech before the Women's National Press Club, Washington, D.C.)

spirit of good will with a determination to eliminate basic differences peacefully, or we turn savage. We who are white must accept the responsibility for rendering the night-rider and his more gentlemanly ally, the friendly neighborhood bigot, impotent.

And those good, responsible people who make up the vast majority of the black community, must repudiate the bigots in their midst. Any other path leads only to the jungle, where those who are outnumbered die.

The President's Commission Report accuses us, you and me, all of us, of white racism. It's a stigma we will live with from now on in our communities and with our fellow citizens unless we prove they're wrong.

You and I know that many of today's problems are the result of prejudice—prejudice that has divided mankind from his very beginning. We know too, that there are those today who continue to spread the poison of bigotry and we cannot ignore them any more than any of us should ignore those others, those millions of others who are determined, and who have been working ceaselessly over the recent years, to make sure that no American ever again will have to tell a child that that child is denied some of the blessings of this land because in some way he is different.

And that's where you and I come in. We can take an interest and we can make a difference. We can insure equal rights and equal opportunity and equal treatment for all our citizens. We can do this by becoming involved in this great problem.

I have been traveling up and down the state of California. I have been going into small meetings, without fanfare, with no press coverage, because that wasn't the purpose of the meetings. I have been quietly meeting with leaders of our minority groups in communities throughout California, and when I say leaders, I don't just necessarily mean the names that you are familiar with that appear in the public print as leaders. I mean those people who are dealing at first hand with the problem in their own neighborhood. Most of the time I have listened to their grievances, their suggestions, their hopes, and their hopelessness.

There is no standard pattern to these meetings. In some, I've met with great bitterness, and in some, I've heard suggestions and information about our own efforts to find solutions. I've learned how our educational system has failed them, how in too many instances we are passing, particularly the student from the minority area, passing the student from grade to grade simply because he's reached the end of the term and not because he's learned anything. And at the end of the line he's handed a certificate or a diploma which is meaningless, because no knowledge goes with it.

He is unable even to read the directions at the beginning of a job training program.

I have learned how our economic system has failed to extend its bounties, as it should, to all who are willing to make an honest effort. I have heard their disillusionment with government programs, promising an instant tomorrow, but designed too often with political opportunism and expediency in mind.

I've been charged, of course, with being opposed to the humanitarian goals because I've vetoed some of those poverty programs. You know, the law does permit the governor to veto such programs and being totally inexperienced, I hadn't discovered that you weren't expected to, so I did. For example, in Ventura County of California, there was a program that on the face of it seemed very sound. It was to put 17 of the hard-core unemployed to work clearing the open-park lands that we have acquired. It sounds all right. But I vetoed the program when I learned that more than half of the budget was going to provide seven administrators to make sure that the seventeen got to work on time.

But that is nothing, compared to one of the programs in Chicago. Eight hundred and seventy-two thousand dollars granted to one of those political gerry-built organizations that was to teach basic reading and arithmetic to dropouts. An inquiring reporter went down after a time to see how the class was coming and he interrupted a crap game.

It was explained that it was recess and then he asked how it was doing? Well, take the faculty, who weren't paid an excessive amount, but who also weren't worked an excessive amount. One of them was in jail for murder, one was in jail for conspiracy to commit murder, three were out on bond awaiting trial for rape, one was out on probation for a burglary conviction. And the director said it was too soon to determine whether the program had been a success.

But these teachers were paid, in addition to their salaries, five dollars a head for each dropout they brought in, and since they were able to offer a dropout forty-five dollars a week plus a family allowance, they found that the best place to pick up an easy five dollars was at the nearest school where they were talking the kids into dropping out and coming over.

Now, this is our fault. Our willingness to accept politics as usual, our easy tolerance for wrong-doing in government, as if this were just standard practice and we should not feel any urge to get angry. And yet, in these meetings, I found responsible, fine men and women of our minority communities, following disappointment after disappointment with a patience that is hard for us to comprehend, scrounging for contributions, trying to keep some of the more effective programs going, after some whim on the part of the government planners had cancelled or reduced them. These people, these people I met with, some of whom confessed they were threatened if they came to such a meeting, they are standing between us and those revolutionaries who believe the only answer left is the last hopeless gesture of the torch and the club.

I don't mean to oversimplify, but I have a belief that jobs are the most important part of this problem. Regardless of all the social problems, regardless of all the things we love to talk about, of equality or opportunity or anything else, the ghetto's walls are economic. It does no good to pass legislation as window-dressing that opens doors if the people you're opening those doors for haven't the price of admission, can't buy the ticket to get in. Of the 17,800 unemployed in the Watts area who were put into jobs by the Chad McClellan program, almost immediately 30% of them moved out of that neighboorhood, proving what the walls consist of in the ghettos.

We have learned something else from these meetings. In spite of the liberal stance of too many of our labor leaders, management today is way ahead of labor with regard to solving this problem.

I know something about employment and I know after 25 years as an officer and a leader of my own union, something of the responsibility of the union to its members when there are not enough jobs to go around.

But I know also, that when less than 3% of the union membership in California comes from our minority communities, there is something wrong and that isn't good enough.

The apprenticeship programs, for instance, are slow to take those who are darker-skinned or who have Spanish surnames. I know, too, California law requires that we as a state do business with equal-opportunity employers and I know that that law is going to be enforced to the letter. We are checking our own civil service regulations. We do not believe that 99.7% of California's jobs require a high school diploma.

In education, we are exploring the possibility of premium pay for the good teachers so that they will be encouraged to take on the hardest jobs where there is the greatest need for their skills. When the physical facilities are needed for youth programs, athletic programs, adult meetings, when Archie Moore, the former champion out in San Diego, has almost two hundred youngsters and he is bringing them up and teaching them self-respect and he has to do it in a little storefront, why should the schoolhouse door be closed at four in the afternoon? Why shouldn't we use those physical facilities and the playground and the meeting room for programs of this kind for the balance of the day and over the weekend and through the summer?

I'll tell you now that I heard no pleas in these meetings for forced bussing or for unnatural integration of children into schools far from their homes. Over and over again, from the people themselves, the plea was for good schooling and discipline in the schools their children are now attending, and, believe it or not, they told me they wanted more education aimed at jobs, at vocational training.

They said to me, "It just isn't true that everybody has to have a college degree to be happy."

There were points in which we were not in agreement.

I hold with government's right to enforce rules guaranteeing that those who do business with the public have an obligation to serve all of the public.

I endorse a law that bans restrictive covenants with regard to housing and I believe that that same law should apply to those who are in the business, the large-scale business of marketing tract homes.

But though I deplore and detest the evil sickness of prejudice and those who practice it, I cannot believe or bring myself to believe that we should open the door to government interference with regard to the individual's right to the disposition of his own personal property, because once that door is opened, government has been granted a right that endangers the very basis of individual freedom, the right to own and the right to possess.

There is a definite limit to what can be accomplished by law or legislation. Inevitably, and this was true in every meeting, we came to the point where the only obvious solution was the responsibility that lies with each one of us, our willingness to become personally involved, willingness to express our disapproval of those who are motivated by prejudice, even while we defend at times their legal rights to indulge in that sickness.

The industrialist must do more than write a memo encouraging the employment of Negroes. Sometimes, we have learned, a memorandum doesn't reach the shop steward or the foreman. We have discovered that if we are to continue with this program of providing jobs, the head of the company, the "top banana," must keep going down clear to the bottom every once in a while to remind them that this is his personal concern, and that it is his wish that they do something about it in each one of these plants and industries.

We have learned in government that many times the policy stops when it leaves our office and gets down to the firing line.

How do you think we feel when we have sent out the word down to our state employment offices and then we find in one of those offices that a man, an instructor, took a young Negro boy in to fill out an application and as they left, having filled it out in one of our California offices, he asked the boy if he had put certain things down that he thought would be helpful and the boy said he forgot? "Well," he said, "let's go back in and add them." And he went back ten minutes later and they couldn't find the application. On a hunch, he walked over to the nearest wastebasket, and they found the application.

School administrators must go out of their way to encourage, and prod, and arm-twist promising minority students, students who don't think that they have a chance of a scholarship and going to college and moving on.

It isn't enough simply to put a little notice up on the board saying that examinations for scholarships are available. They have got to take a personal interest and see that those individuals have their chance.

Yes, all of us have to spend a little less time trying to be our brother's keeper and start trying to be our brother's brother. We are embarked on such a course in California.

Not because of any talk of a long, hot summer or a long, hot any-other-period of the year; this is not a crash program.

We are doing what we're doing because it is morally right to do it and it's a good thing to do.

The funny thing is, it is good from every angle. It is good business. Industry in America today needs men and women. It is crying for them to fill skilled jobs and here we have a community filled with men and women who need only the skills to fill those jobs. The alternative is to perpetuate poverty, keeping them on the dole at our expense. With jobs they become productive citizens, sharing the burden of government with the rest of us and making it easier to solve the rest of the social problems. If we can raise our minority communities to just the average level of purchasing power of the rest of the majority community, we have a potential market for our free enterprise system that is equal to or even greater than the foreign market, whose loss threatens our prosperity at this very moment. That French philosopher so often quoted by all after-luncheon and after-dinner speakers, De Tocqueville, came to this country more than a hundred years ago, searching for the secret of America's greatness and finally found it. He said America is great because America is good, and he said if America ever ceases to be good, America will cease to be great.

Now, I am sure that some of what I have said has sounded very strange to some of you, coming from one who has in the kindest words been termed a conservative and by some has been charged with being willing to eat his young.

It shouldn't sound so strange, though. There is a Democratic state legislator out there in California, a black American, who represents the Watts area, Bill Green. He is a liberal, and he says, "One thing California and the nation have to realize is that the black community and the conservative community are coming much closer together. Liberals tend to intellectualize the question out of existence."

Well, I personally deplore the use of such labels as conservative, moderate, or liberal, or any other. I prefer to think that we are coming to a realization that those who look only to government for the answers have failed for some years to recognize the great potential force for good among those who instead have placed their faith in the doctrine of the individual.

We are dealing with individuals. Each one of them—they are not a mass problem. Each one of them is unique as we are unique and each one of them is uttering the same cry. It has been uttered by mankind since the very beginning. That cry from within that wants him to be recognized as having human dignity and independence. The American dream that we have nursed for so long in this country and neglected so much lately is not that every man must be level with every other man. The American dream is that every man must be free to become whatever God intends he should become. The restoration and the perpetuation of that dream is the greatest challenge confronting every one of us today.

6. TAKE THE JUDGES OUT OF POLITICS

LAW DAY is celebrated on May 1—the same day that lawless communism celebrates the anniversary of the Red Revolution.

The contrast is even greater than it might seem at first glance. Communism by definition is a government of men—not of laws. It is the very antithesis of what our founding fathers had in mind when they laboriously and carefully designed our Constitution.

They feared a strong, central government, because a strong central government is a threat to personal liberty. But, even more, they feared a government of men. Because they knew from first-hand experience that government by men is government uncontrolled and that that is tyranny.

They knew that no man was safe in his house, or in his property or in his person if his rights, personal or property, depended upon the whims of men or of a man. They set out to prevent this from happening. And the job they did

(Transcript of talk before the University of Southern California Law Day luncheon.)

through the document they wrote was the best in the history of man.

They were not infallible and the Constitution—great as it is—is not a perfect document. It can work only so long as a people truly desire to be free, only so long as men refuse to subject themselves to the rule of other men.

The man who said "eternal vigilance is the price of liberty" was not speaking lightly or tritely. Eternal vigilance is indeed the price of liberty, and that price is not too high to pay. But liberty, without law, without legal safeguards is not and cannot be liberty in the long run. It becomes, instead, license, revolution and anarchy. It leads, without qualification, to mob rule and from there to the rule of the many by the few. And these in turn establish or disestablish law as they see fit, or ignore the law and rule by fiat or edict.

What free men must achieve in order to remain free is a delicate balance wherein some liberty is sacrificed in order that the remainder may be preserved. This cannot be successfully achieved or long maintained unless those who make the laws are answerable to the people and unless the people are willing and able to hold them answerable.

We have jealously guarded the concept that ours is a government of laws, not of men. But we must always remember that the laws are written by men, interpreted by men and changed by men. And that men are judged under the law by other men. Because of this, Americans have an obligation to themselves and to those who will come after them to see that those who write the laws, those who interpret them and those who judge under them are men of ability, men of honor and men who are fair-minded.

Now a governor can recommend laws and execute them, but he cannot make them under our system. Nor can he elect or appoint those who do. And, with the exception of his clemency power, the governor cannot judge under the law, but he can, in fact under our system, he must, appoint those who do judge.

In many ways this is the most awesome power a governor has. Because, while judges must in theory be approved by a vote of the people, in actuality, a man appointed judge, with rare exceptions, has a lifetime job. An inherent weakness in our system is that it is nearly impossible for the average citizen to have all the factual information necessary to make an intelligent decision in voting for a judge, and therefore, he usually votes for the incumbent.

This, as I say, places an awesome responsibility and power in the hands of the governor. He in effect, controls the administration of justice, through the men he chooses. Justice can be good, bad or indifferent, depending on the judge and on the man who appoints the judge.

There are many in California, including many in the legislature, who prefer our present system. They recognize that a governor can and may make bad appointments to the bench. They recognize that governors can, and many have, made appointments to the bench as political payoffs. But they feel sincerely that over a period of years, the system balances out and that in the main the quality of the courts is high. Some of these men frankly feel that the appointment of judges is better off in the hands of a governor than it is in the hands of anyone else.

Their reasoning is clear. In California, a party seldom remains in control of the governor's office more than one or two terms at a time. This means that each party, under a system that encourages the political appointments of judges, will wind up with its share.

I suspect this is true. But I submit that this is not the way to improve the quality of our appointees to the bench. Nor is a party balance necessary to justice in our criminal courts. I submit to you that justice should not be political. The theme of Law Day this year is that "no man is above the law and no man is below it . . ." I would add that all men are entitled to equal justice under it.

I believe that using our courts as political plums in a

spoils system is no way to assure the first—or to achieve the second. That is why I am disappointed that the Senate Judiciary Committee killed for this session legislation introduced at my request that would have taken the appointment of judges out of politics.

During the campaign I promised we would seek action in this area. That promise was made in a hundred different speeches. The reaction of one hundred different crowds made it obvious that the people want assurance that California justice is not justice diluted by partisan politics. The appointment of dozens of judges, many of which must be regarded as political payoffs, by a lame-duck governor last fall and winter, did nothing to build the confidence of Californians in our political system or in our administration of justice. My mail reflected this and reflected even more strongly than during the campaign the people's wish for something better.

Because of my beliefs, because of the promises I made and because it is obviously the people's desire, I sent to the Legislature the bill that was killed. Actually, the bill would take a constitutional amendment to become effective and therefore, after legislative approval it would have to be submitted to a vote of the people. I am sorry the Senate Judiciary Committee did not give the people the right to make that decision.

That bill, known as the California Judicial Selection Act, I believed, would once and for all take the appointment of judges out of the political arena. Under the bill a judicial nominating commission would have been created, consisting of the Chief Justice of the State Supreme Court, two attorneys appointed by the State Bar and three lay citizens named by the governor. That commission would review the names of those proposed by any person for appointment to the Appellate Courts. After review, the commission would submit at least two names to the governor who would then make an appointment from that list.

At the trial court level the commission would be augmented by three persons from the community where a vacancy existed. One would be a member of the local bar designated by the local bar president, one would be a judge and a third would be a lay person named by the governor.

When a vacancy occurred the governor would be required to submit at least three names to the commission and the commission would in turn recommend from this list at least two names back to the governor. The governor would then appoint a judge from among those names. If the commission were unable to recommend at least two persons from the governor's list he would be required to furnish additional names. This would assure that the governor must submit the names of qualified attorneys as possible bench appointees.

There is one other key provision to this bill. It would change the election procedures to further take the naming of judges out of politics. Instead of making the election of municipal and superior court judges contested races, voters would be asked only to vote yes—or no—as they now do on the Appellate Court level. If the vote were no, the judge would not be re-elected and a new judge would be named under the appointive system I mentioned a moment ago.

Let me say now that I think what I have proposed is what the people want and what in the interests of justice, the people deserve. I promise unequivocally that I will resubmit this legislation for as long as necessary to have it enacted into law.

7.   WHAT PRICE PEACE?

NOVEMBER 11 was named Armistice Day in observance of the silencing of guns in a war that was fought to end all wars and to make the world safe for democracy.

Now this day has been renamed because other Americans have died, and died for noble causes. Twenty-odd years after that war to end wars, the sons of the Doughboy were G.I.'s in World War II, and they fought for our freedoms. They created an organization to end wars, and we have known very little peace since. They and their younger brothers and even their sons fought again in Korea, and today another generation of young Americans is dying in Vietnam.

We at home are torn with dissension and we accuse each other, trying to find blame and place blame for why this should be. There are those among us who charge that the fault is ours—that we are the aggressors—that peace could come to the world if we would but change our ways. To each solution that is offered, to every alternative, they plaintively cry "there are no simple answers to these complex prob-

(From a Veteran's Day Address, North Albany Junior High School, Oregon.)

lems." Is it possible that the answer is, in truth, simple, but one that demands too much—one that is simply too hard for too many of us to accept? Is it possible, perhaps, that peace has become so dear and life so sweet that some would buy it at the price of chains and slavery?

Let us start with the assumption that everyone in the world wants peace. We pick up our daily press and almost every issue carries stories of those who want peace. We know that our clergy, with the greatest of sincerity, urge that we pray for peace. (Of course we must be careful not to do this in a public schoolroom.) Businessmen form organizations to strive for peace.

With all this universal demand and all this concentration on peace, why, then, should it be so impossible to achieve? In all of history, one can find few, if any, instances where the people have started a war. War is the province of government, and therefore the more autocratic government is, the more centralized, the more totalitarian, the more government can direct and control the will of the people—the greater the chance for war.

We hear the cry for peace everywhere, but another word seems absent—no voices seem to be crying "freedom." How long since we have heard about that? Each year we observe a Captive Nations Day. At one time, pronouncements on that day here in our own land anticipated the future freedom of those now held captive and enslaved. But more and more, we have diluted that theme, until now we use the day to speak of peace with no mention of freedom. Is it possible that while we are sorry for the captives, we do not want to offend the captors? If we have the courage to face reality, peace is not so difficult to come by. We can have peace by morning if we do not mind the price. What is blocking the quest for peace? We all know the answer even if some in high places are reluctant to voice it.

A totalitarian force in the world has made plain its goal is world domination. This has been reiterated by Nikita

Khrushchev and by the present rulers of Russia. Each one has stated that they will not retreat one inch from the Marxian concept of a one-world socialist state. So, all we have to do, if peace is so dear, is surrender. Indeed, not even that— just announce that we are giving up war and the tools of war, we are going to mind our own business, we will not fight with anyone for any reason, and we shall have peace.

Why are we so reluctant to do this? Because there is a price we will not pay for peace, and it has to do with freedom. We want peace, but only if we can be free at the same time. Too many of us remember a few years back when the tanks rumbled through Hungary and over the bodies of the freedom fighters. And then above the echoes of the last few shots came that final radioed plea to humanity: "People of the world, help us. People of Europe, whom we once defended against the attacks of Asiatic barbarians, listen now to the alarm bells ring. People of the civilized world, in the name of liberty and solidarity, we are asking you to help. The light vanishes, the shadows grow darker hour by hour. Listen to our cry."

And sometimes when the wind is right, it seems we can still hear that cry and we find ourselves wondering if the conscience of man will be hearing that cry a thousand years from now. There are those in our midst who do believe we can bring peace by the unilateral action I have described—by simply refusing to fight. Please believe me, it would be folly for us to challenge their sincere belief that we can end the cold war simply by convincing the enemy of our good intentions, and that it isn't necessary that we ask him to give up his plan for imposing his will upon the world. But we can challenge their lack of touch with reality.

As I said earlier, we all share in their desire for peace. Not one of us will take second place to any other in willingness to do everything possible to achieve peace. It is precisely because we do want peace that we plead for a review of history. Page after page has been bloodied by the reckless adventures of power-hungry monarchs and dictators who mistook man's love of peace for weakness.

How many nations have backed down the road of good intentions to end up against a wall of no retreat with the only choice fight or surrender? We do not repudiate man's dream of peace. We must not. It is a good dream and one we share with all men for the dream is as old as man himself.

But we do repudiate an attempt to achieve that dream by methods disproven by all of our past experience, methods played against the background music of Neville Chamberlain's umbrella tapping its sorry way to the slaughter of a generation of young men.

Nor can we safely rest the case of freedom with the United Nations as it is presently constituted. Not until reconstruction of this organization puts realistic power in the hands of those nations which must, through size and strength, be ultimately responsible for world order, can we submit questions affecting our national interest to the UN and be confident of a fair hearing.

I realize there are those who will charge we offer an alternative of narrow nationalism and chip-on-the-shoulder sabre rattling, that we endanger the world and bring closer the dread day of the bomb.

Go back a few years and recall another time of crisis. This time the Red Chinese were threatening to invade the offshore islands and Formosa. The world tensed and we heard the familiar terror talk that any action of any kind would bring on World War III. And then another voice was heard speaking in a tone we have not heard for too long a time in this land of ours. Dwight David Eisenhower said: "They'll have to crawl over the 7th fleet to do it."

The invasion of Formosa did not take place; no young men died; and World War III did not follow.

By contrast, we listened to those who said Laos would be the wrong war in the wrong place at the wrong time. So we backed down to buy peace and we bought Vietnam.

Armistice Day is not being honored in Vietnam. The set of enemies who confront Americans in Southeast Asia are half a world removed in space—and perhaps even a whole century removed in time—from the collection of enemies whom we faced in that war to end wars in Europe half a century ago. And if we believe the more pessimistic political scientists, the war which we fight now in Asia is one in which our enemy will never accept an armistice. He will fight on and on, we are told, until the United States gives up and withdraws in weariness and failure.

What about the solemn lessons that Americans were supposed to have learned from all the wars, great and small, which they have fought through the past half a century?

From those tremendous campaigns across Europe and Africa; and on the seas and under the seas and in the skies; and in Asia and among the Pacific Islands?

From the billions and billions of dollars beyond counting that have been spent on weapons and munitions, and on moving armies and fleets and air forces across the face of the earth —sums vast enough to support whole civilizations?

And what has happened to the warrior skills that came to Americans from experience in wars—experience unwanted and unsought, but unmatched nevertheless?

We Americans have had one general and continuing experience outside our waters these past 50 years. It is the experience of fighting wars, and trying to prevent wars. And yet, at this dismal juncture, somehow we are unable or at least unwilling to bring to terms, or force to an armistice, a ramshackle water buffalo economy with a gross national budget hardly equal to that of Pascagaula.

What has gone wrong? What has happened to our knowledge of politics and power?

Where did the American strategic responses in Southeast Asia begin to go awry?

I, for one, find it strange that two of the nine Justices of the Supreme Court should now assert in public that the legality

of the American military operations in that part of the world
should be reviewed by that Court.

If there are indeed true grounds for suspicion of illegal
acts or actions, as Justices Douglas and Potter seem to imply,
what a monstrous crime that would be! Here are more than
500,000 fresh troops being sent forth across the Pacific in
their youthful innocence. If they are encouraged in illegal
acts then scores of generals and admirals must be accessories
before and after the fact. And if a crime has been committed,
whose crime would it be? The President's? McNamara's?
Or the members of Congress who passed the Tonkin Gulf
Resolution which the President insists provided him with
legal sanctions? And how would Justices Potter and Douglas measure the offense, if an offense there be? Would the
war-making be felony? Or a misdemeanor? And what punishment would they prescribe to fit such a crime?

It is impossible to imagine anything sillier.

Maybe it could be argued as a legalism that the Administration of the hour has in fact misled the people and taken them
wrongly into war. That would be a matter between the Executive Branch and the people. That is one thing, and I
am not necessarily disposed to hold with either Justice on the
point. The other thing is, of course, whether American forces
should be in Vietnam at all. Let me make my own position
clear. I believe that the United States has work to do and a
place to fill in the Pacific, and that we must not stop fighting
until the security of our allies has been assured in freedom
and independence. This war, in other words, had to be
fought, even if it is not yet called a war. which it is. But I also
hold that we got into it in an altogether strange and even
mysterious way, and that is the cause of much of the confusion and acrimony and anguish among us.

The fundamental error was made just about seven years
ago and that first year, 1961, was a bad year for the United
State's power position in the world. It was the year of the
incredible botch at the Bay of Pigs; of Khrushchev's cold

and calculated affront to our President at their meeting in Vienna; of the ominous start of another Soviet crunch at Berlin; of the earth-shaking Soviet breach of the nuclear test moratorium; of the first large, vicious armed attacks by the Viet Cong on the South Vietnamese villages; and of the breaking by the North Vietnamese of the promised neutrality of Laos.

The year 1961 was, on the fact of the record, the year when Soviet Russia in alliance with Ho Chi Minh in Asia, clearly decided to test, at places of their choosing, the nerve and stamina of a new Administration in Washington . . .

We decided not to stand in Laos. We accepted the occupation of Eastern Laos by the Pathet Lao Communists, who, like the Viet Cong, were and remain a nationalist front for Hanoi. We made what in the international jargon of diplomacy is called a political and strategic retreat. But this retreat was not described to the rest of us as a retreat. On the contrary, the compact which thus split Laos into three parts was celebrated as a great feat of statesmanship.

What it did, of course, in the Eastern one-third of Laos was to open uncontested access to the corridors in South Vietnam from the north. It is known to our fighting men as the Ho Chi Minh trail.

The sequence of American actions thereafter is clear, even if the strategical reasoning is not.

The prime recommendation of the Taylor-Rostow team was to raise the strength of the United States military mission in South Vietnam from a few hundred men— (about 700 men, actually)—to some 15,000 men. The American forces already in the country were not combat troops. On the contrary, they were concerned almost exclusively with the chore of training and equipping a small South Vietnamese army, itself without experience and tradition in war. The additional troops who were sent in also were charged with continuing the training and equipping, but they were to do more of it faster. From that point on, nothing went right.

The very people we were trying to help kept warning that
an aggression was in the making, and that the appeasement
in Laos would have the fatal effect of making South Vietnam vulnerable. But Washington simply was not listening.
Well, it has been a dreary matter of addition ever since.
There were a mere 700 or so training troops at the start.
Then 15,000 more and then the combat formations—first by
regiments—then by brigades, and finally by divisions. And
now, only six years later, more than 500,000 American troops
are there.

From the start, it was a case of being too late with too little, while tipping our hand to the enemy so that he always
knew in advance what we proposed.

The strategy has been justified with a quotation from another General named Polybius. That strategy holds:

"It is not the purpose of war to annihilate those who pro-
voke it, but to cause them to mend their ways."

Polybius was a Roman who wrote on war 2,000 years before our twentieth-century invention of "wars of national
liberation."

In any case, neither Polybius, or even General Maxwell
Taylor, seem to have provided a satisfactory answer. Wars,
or politics conducted in the form of war, simply cannot be
won or settled that way.

And the cost of trying to get Ho to improve his manners
keeps going up and up—to more than $30 billion a year.
Worse still, the options now open to us from the existing plat-
form of strategy grow more difficult.

Some say the war cannot be won by force and that the
bombing should be stopped. Stop the bombing, and we will
only encourage the enemy to do his worst. A Marine General
reported that in one bombing pause, his men counted 150
truck convoys and more than 300 sampans bringing up sup-
plies. Some others hold for a closing of Haiphong and even an
Inchon-type landing. The feasibility of such actions is a
matter for the generals and admirals to decide—a profes-

sional judgment. But the military can only advise. It is for the government and the people, and only they, to decide what is to be done with such advice, if anything is to be done at all.

The one thing that is sure in this situation is that we Americans must finally make up our minds as a people whether we want to carry the war through to a conclusion, or give up.

We Americans who live on the West Coast do not look on the Pacific as an alien sea, or upon Asia as a feared or alien shore. For generations, we have treaded across this ocean, and now the jets go back and forth. In a very real sense, we are a Pacific people, as we are also an Atlantic people. Senator Fulbright and Mr. Walter Lippmann to the contrary, we are not —nor can we ever be—indifferent to what happens there. And least of all can we turn away from an aggression which seeks to crush free and independent nations and, toward that end, would eject the protective American influence from the Western Pacific.

Isn't it time that we admitted we are in Vietnam because our national interest demands that we take a stand there now so we won't have to take a stand later on our own beaches?

Isn't it time that we either win this war or tell the American people why we can't? Isn't it time to recognize the great immorality of sending our neighbors' sons to die with the hope we can do so without angering the enemy too much? Isn't this a throwback to those jungle tribes sacrificing a few of their select young on a heathen altar to keep the volcano from exploding?

The war in Vietnam must be fought through to victory, meaning first, an end to North Vietnam aggression, and second, an honorable and safe peace for our South Vietnam friends. We have been patient long enough and our patience wears thin. This is the way to peace and it is a way in keeping with our basic principles.

Probably no society has ever been founded completely on

the principal of individualism, but certainly our government and our system has come closer than man has ever come in all the history of man's relation to man. Ours is the concept that an individual's rights are inviolate, and thus we are deeply disturbed at the idea that young men can be asked to die for a cause unless that cause is worth winning and worth involving the total effort of all of us collectively.

8. THE GENERATION GAP

THIRTY-FIVE years and a few months ago, I got my first college degree.

As far as students today are concerned, that makes it definite I am *not* of their generation. There are those with differing political views who would go even further and place me as far back as the Ice Age—some even further, to the time of McKinley.

Some, however, can bear witness that 35 years are like 35 minutes, so clear and fresh is memory. No matter how much today's students may want to believe this, their imaginations are not quite up to it. They will just have to wait and find out for themselves. But they will find out.

There is a tendency in today's world to put more than years between us. Somehow, as humans, we have been stratified into a horizontal society instead of vertical. Layers of humanity are separated into age groups from pre-school to those the social tinkerers refer to as senior citizens. And somehow we are losing our ability to establish communications

(From a talk at Eureka College, Illinois, Sept. 28, 1967.)

between layers. What is even worse, there is a growing hostility between these layers.

It is an unnatural situation. Humanity is vertically structured. The teen-ager will become the young married or junior executive, and in turn, the middle aged and eventually the senior citizen. Each one of us will take his faults and virtues, his pluses and minuses through the years, being at all times the sum total of all he has experienced.

This separation into horizontal layers makes no sense at all. What of this talk that no one over 30 understands the youth of today? If this is true, then what happens when they reach 30? Does youth suddenly join us and quit understanding those who have not quite reached the magic age?

Each generation is critical of its predecessor. As the day nears when classroom and playing field must give way to the larger arena with its problems of inequality and human misunderstanding, it is easy to look at those in that arena and demand to know why the problems remain unsolved. We who preceded asked that question of those who preceded us and another younger generation will ask it in turn.

I hope there will be less justification for the question when it is youth's turn to answer. What I am trying to say is that no generation has failed completely, nor will this one succeed completely.

But don't get me wrong. When the generation of which I am a part leaves the stage, history will record that seldom has any generation fought harder or paid a higher price for freedom.

We have known three wars and now a fourth, a cataclysmic world-wide depression that toppled governments and re-shaped the map. And, because we could not find the single cure-all for man's inhumanity to man or the answer to human frailty, we have downgraded our performance and confused our young people as well as ourselves.

It is easy to point to the failures and talk of the mess of our times, and even to promise to do better. But for the record, since we are the generation that exploded the atomic bomb and brought a permanent terror to the world, we also harnessed the atom for peaceful purposes. And some of those peaceful purposes in medicine and industrial power have brought man to the threshhold of a fabulous era.

We have defeated polio and tuberculosis and a host of plague diseases that held even more terror for mankind than the threat of the bomb. It is fairly certain that your generation and ours will overlap in defeating cancer.

Point an accusing finger and list smog, water pollution, poverty, civil rights, inequality of opportunity. We still seek the answers, and while many of us disagree as to the solutions, we were the ones who faced up to the problems and charged ourselves with finding the answers. No one in public life fails to treat with them.

This horizontal stratification has led to lateral communication and it is highly essential that we restore vertical dialogue if not an outright recognition of the naturalness and rightness of a vertical structuring of society.

How well do young people understand those whose defect is being age 30 plus? Can you possibly believe your fathers who knew the savagery of World War II, or your grandfathers who came of age in the muddy trenches of the Great War, could possibly have an affection for war? . . . That we would callously send our sons to war?

Permit me here to build at least a foot bridge between the age groups of parent and child, remembering that bridges are open to traffic both ways.

That fellow with the thickening waist and the thinning hair who is sometimes unreasonable about your allowance or letting you have the car . . . his life seems a little dull to you now as he reports for his daily 9-to-5 chores or looks forward to lowering a golf handicap, or catching a fish no one wants to eat.

I wish today's undergraduates could have known him a few years back on a landing craft at Normandy or Tarawa or on

a weekend pass in Peoria. He was quite a guy. Winston
Churchill said he was the only man in the world who could
laugh and fight at the same time. General Marshall called
him our secret weapon. He hated war more than he hated the
enemy, but he did what had to be done.

A few years after the end of World War II, I was in a little
pub in rural England. The motherly soul who was waiting
on trade figured out I was an American (for the life of me, I
don't know how). She began to reminisce. "During the war,"
she said, "some of your chaps were stationed just across the
road. They used to come in here and have song-fests. They
called me Mom and my husband Pop. It was Christmas Eve
and we were here all alone when the door burst open and
there they were with presents for us." She paused for a tear
or two and then said: "Big strappin' lads they was from a
place called 'Ioway'."

I know those over-30 fellows probably don't tell it very
well, but they all knew what it was like to dream, to say good-
bye to a girl and wonder when, if ever, they would see her
again. They missed a world that let things like that happen,
and swore they would do better when they got back and
were running the show.

Today there is great concern among my generation that an
era of permissiveness has resulted in unrest among our young
people. But just to keep things in balance, there is a widespread feeling among our young people that no one over 30
understands them. I would like to point out understanding is
a two-way street. I would think that for our young people intellectual curiosity alone would prompt the students to do a
little research in that older generation. After all there is one
attractive thing we have to look at; we are the only ones in
this confrontation who have been both ages.

Now it might be reassuring to the young to know as they
start to catch up with us, that growing old isn't bad when
you consider the alternative. You know, I have no apology

to make for our generation. Mistakes we've made to be sure. We haven't achieved all that we would like to have achieved. But still we are a generation that has lived through three world wars and a cataclysmic depression that shook the very foundation of our nation. I believe basically our generation has remained true to our belief in simple justice. We have remained compassionate to those less fortunate. We have stood firm in our duties to those who would come after us. At the same time, let me say, on behalf of the younger generation, I think all of us are frank to admit they have more knowledge than we had at their age, are far better informed, and are far more aware of the winds that are swirling about and bringing changes in this world of ours. So I think with good will on both sides there are plenty of areas where we can get together.

You are concerned with us and what seems to be hypocrisy and lack of purpose on our part. And we in turn are concerned about you, seeing a rising spirit of unrest, aimlessness and drifting, a feeling of rebellion without a real cause that results sometimes in meaningless but violent actions. Now let me make it plain. I am aware that all of you are unfairly suspect because of a very small percentage of dissidents.

Nevertheless, you do seek a purpose and a meaning to life and apparently we have failed to give it to you. But, again, our failure was not one of bad intent.

We are the classic example of giving to you what we never had . . . from TV to Little League. But I am afraid we shortchanged you on responsibilities or the right to earn for yourselves.

All too often, because we had to earn, we wanted to give. Our motives have been laudable, but our judgment has been bad. "No," was either a dirty word or dropped from our vocabulary.

Some time ago in Newport, California, a row of luxurious ocean-front homes was threatened by an abnormally high tide and heavy surf. All through the day and night, volunteers worked, piling sandbags, in an effort to save these homes. Local TV stations, aware of the drama, covered the struggle. It was about 2 a.m. when one newscaster grabbed a young fellow in his teens, attired only in wet trunks. He had been working all day and night—one of several hundred of his age group. No, he did not live in one of the houses they were trying to save, and yes, he was cold and tired. The newscaster inevitably got around to why. The answer was so poignant, such an indictment of so many of us, it should be on a billboard across the nation. He said: "Well, I guess it's the first time we've ever felt like we were needed."

But this young generation is needed, we need your courage, your idealism, your new and untried viewpoint. You know more than we did, you are brighter, better informed, even healthier. And because human kind *is* vertically structured, we can take a little credit for that. But, you want a purpose, a cause, a banner to follow and we owe you that.

A few years ago, a national magazine did a series of articles by prominent people including a president, a vice-president and distinguished statesmen. Each wrote his idea of what our national purpose was. Somehow, nothing very exciting or profound resulted from these articles. I have always felt it was because they tried to invent something we already have and have had for 200 years. Our national purpose is to unleash the full talent and genius of the individual, not to create mass movements with the citizenry subjecting themselves to the whims of the state. Here, as nowhere in the world, we are established to provide the ultimate in individual freedom consistent with law and order.

Eureka College is dedicating a library. This would not be possible if humanity were indeed horizontally structured. This dedication began more than a hundred years ago when Ben Major struck an axe into a tree and said on this spot we will build our school. According to history, the wagon train had not even been unloaded and homes had not been built, but a site was chosen for a school.

Walnut Grove Academy became Eureka College because others followed in Ben Major's footsteps, giving and building, not for themselves, but for others who would come later and take their places higher up on the vertical column of mankind.

This library exists because Wesley and Clinton Melick have thought not in horizontal lines of just their associates in time. You want a purpose, something to believe in? You might try resolving that you will contribute something to generations unborn—a handhold above your own achievement so that another generation can climb higher and achieve more.

When I suggest that we turn to books, to the accumulated knowledge of the past, I am not suggesting that we turn back the clock or retreat into some dim yesterday that we remember only with nostalgia, if at all. But we must learn from yesterday to have a better tomorrow.

We are beset by problems in a complex world; we are confused by those who tell us only new and untried ways offer hope. The answers to the problems of mankind will be found in this building by those who have the desire to find them and perception enough to recognize them.

There will be the knowledge of Aristotle, Plato and Socrates, and from the vantage point of history, their mistakes. We can look back and see where pure democracy became as dictatorial as a sultan, and majority rule without protection for the minority became mob rule.

One of mankind's problems is that we keep repeating the same errors. For some place every generation, two plus two has added up to three, or in another place, five—four seems to elude some of us. This has happened in my generation and I predict without smugness, it will happen to yours.

I think that this is the significance of this library. The fact that we can use it to rechart our course, not into the great un-known, but onto paths that are clear and which, if followed, can show us how to cope with the new problems that always confront each generation and can lead us, as a people, on to continued greatness.

9. HOW SICK IS MEDICARE?

MEDICARE programs are in fact sicker than the people they are expected to aid. Certainly, that is true here in our own state of California, where unless Medi-Cal is revised and revamped, it not only can, but most assuredly will, bankrupt our state, and in a very few years.

I was raised in a small town back in the Midwest and I was in poverty before it became popular, before the rich folks got hold of it. My father always said, "It's no disgrace to be poor, but it might as well be." Perhaps one of the differences between then and now is that I only know now that we were poor then; the government wasn't telling us at the time.

But I don't believe that just giving the poor a handout is of any great service to them, whether it be money or medical care. And I don't believe that the bulk of those who aspire to a better life want just a handout. They may need a step up, a helping hand, but they want it so they can do better for themselves.

(Excerpts from speech at Governors' Conference on Medicaid, San Francisco.)

There is no question of our responsibility to those less fortunate. I don't think any one of us would retreat from that responsibility. But, we also have a responsibility to those who make that helping hand possible.

There are those among us today who have established the idea that welfare is an inalienable right of the recipient. But what of the right of those who work and earn, and share the fruit of their toil to make welfare possible, and those who earn their own way, pay their own doctors and provide for public welfare with their earnings? These people are restrained in the amount of care they can afford for themselves.

The minor illness, the cold, the cut finger, is treated at home and then they call in a doctor when their reason tells them the trip is justified.

The key to the problem is that these same people are now providing medical care for their fellow citizens, more comprehensive than they can afford for themselves. With the best intentions in establishing this program, we have created a situation where there is no restraint on those who are receiving Medi-Cal. They are free to seek help for the most trivial of ailments simply because it represents no cost to themselves.

While the overshelming majority of doctors are honorable and have a long history of extending the best of care to those who seek it, still, as in any profession, there are some who can't resist a good thing and so in this program we have no restraint, no way of checking on the doctor who has the patient return for two or three checkups on these trivial ailments. We have no way of curbing the hypochondriac who has, at public expense, an examination and then goes on from doctor to doctor trying to find one who will tell him what he wants to hear.

These are technical problems, problems of administration, of regulations, and I cannot believe they are beyond our ability to solve them. But, I do believe that in fulfilling responsibility to the less fortunate, we must make sure that the working men and women of our nation and our states do not provide better health services for the less fortunate than they are able to provide for themselves.

I believe also that government, in making provision for health services for the poor, should make maximum use of the voluntary organizations. Any Medicare program will have a heavy influence on private sector health services. Therefore, in developing the programs we need we must remember we have an obligation to preserve the voluntary hospital system, the private health insurance programs and the integrity of doctors who have given this nation the best medical care in the world under the private enterprise system.

We have a responsibility to face up to the fact that, in those nations who have turned to nationalized programs or socialized medicine, they cannot possibly match the quality of medical care that we have developed under a contrary system. Of course, the answer is not the opposite extreme of no government involvement at all. It is, instead, a partnership of private effort and governmental activity—a system in which those with true need are helped and the rest of us permitted to help also.

We are living in a period of rapid change. It is obvious that medical science will continue to unfold opportunities for better health services for our people. As these opportunities appear, we in state government will have a particular responsibility and that is to organize government's activities in these areas so that strong leadership and efficient administration can be provided without disrupting the voluntary system which has brought health care in the United States to the standards we enjoy today.

I know the problems are many and complicated. But they are not beyond our capacity to solve and certainly we are obliged to solve them. We cannot meet the problem of part of our citizens by unduly penalizing another part.

10. THE LAST ISLAND OF FREEDOM

IN THESE first few weeks I have learned the truth of an old, old story.

It has to do with a man and his son in an ancient land. He was leading a burro down the road, and they met a man who said to them, "This is ridiculous for both of you to be walking on this hot day, with that beast of burden there. Don't you know that his duty is to carry you? At least one of you should be riding."

So the father heeded his advice and put his son on the back of the burro and they proceeded down the road until they met another man who again referred to the heat of the day and said that the burro was a beast of burden and, he said, "It is ridiculous for you to be walking, you both should be riding. The burro is capable of that." So they both got aboard the little burro.

Finally they met a third man, and he said, "How can you do that on such a hot day? Look at the size of you, the two of

(*Address before convention of National Sand and Gravel Assn., Los Angeles, Feb. 8, 1967.*)

you should be carrying the burro." And the very willing man got down and his son got down and they tied the burro's feet together, put a pole through and put it on their shoulders and proceeded on their way until they crossed a little bridge over a raging torrent.

And with this concentrated load, the bridge collasped and they were plunged into the water. The father and son managed to make it to shore all right, but the burro, with its feet tied together, drowned. And the moral is, you can lose your burro by trying to please everybody.

Somebody once said that there is nothing particularly difficult about business. You just make some stuff and sell it for more than it costs you—this, of course, brings me to that moment when a speaker is concerned lest it seem, in what he says, that he is trying to give advice. And this I don't want to do.

There was a little girl, who wrote a three-line essay in school one day and the essay was on Socrates. She said, "Socrates was a Greek Scholar. He went around giving people advice; they poisoned him."

I have been protesting the growth of government for a number of years, protesting and expressing a concern lest government should become so complex it will be unmanageable. Now, there are some who perhaps would believe that now with the recent change of occupation, I would change my tune. But I want you to know that I am just as frightened of government, even though I am now part of it, as I had been back through these many years, and I believe being frightened and concerned with the growth of government is legitimate. Certainly there is a foundation for our concern.

You know that there is a door in the nation's capitol, in the General Services Administration, and the sign on this door, I think, illustrates what can happen with government. It says: General Services Administration, Region Three, Public Building Service Building, Management Division, Utility Room, Custodian.

It's the broom closet.

But as if that isn't enough—perhaps some of you have heard me tell about another item I found one day. There is a 20-man unit or committee in the Pentagon, and this unit —these 20 men—bear this title collectively: Input Reparations Section of the Report Reparations Branch of the Operational Division of the Army Information and Data Systems Command of the Office of the Army Chief of Staff. Now, knowing Washington for reducing all agencies to initials, and then coining an abbreviated title or word spelled out by those initials, like SAC or NATO, I couldn't help but conjure up what might happen with some proud wife of one of those 20 men on that committee, casually telling an old school chum where her husband works . . . you can hear her hanging over the fence, saying that he is busy down at. . . .

Now, I realize that this subject of government and government's function is, of course, controversial . . . highly controversial and we have been rapidly shaping into kind of two sides in regard to the philosophical discussion. But I am also prepared to say that, after a few weeks in government, I wish in the legitimate debate that can take place between these philosophies, that people would make sure they know what errands you are on and what you are trying to do. I refer to a little story that took place in an airplane.

There was a pilot, commercial airline, and a moment after they were airborne, he comes on the microphone and tells everyone how glad the airline is to have them there, how pleasant the flight will be, and then says, "Now, if you will just sit back and enjoy yourselves" . . . and he neglected to turn off the mike, and proceeded to add: "if I had a beer and a blonde, I would be happy too." And in the rear of the plane the stewardess, a very attractive young girl, by coincidence heard this, and alarmed, started to rush to the front of the plane. As she passed a sweet little, elderly lady sitting on an aisle seat, the lady said, "Miss, you forgot the beer."

There is a great deal of speculation about what the last

election meant. Now I don't mean just in California, as I am beginning to wonder about that myself, but I mean nation-wide. And you have heard all sorts of theories advanced. We have heard stories about various kinds of backlash and this and that. But I've got my own view, seriously, as to what I think took place in November, 1967.

And frankly, I find it encouraging, because I think the people last November 8 all across this country voted *against*. I think they vetoed a great deal of what's been going on. I think they voted against the idea that we can go on spending more than we take in without someday having the bill pro-rated to our individual share and presented to each one of us for payment.

I think the people voted against distorting compassion . . . compassion that has led us, as a nation, to distribute the goods produced in the country widely among our people —more widely than has been known in any society hereto-fore created by man. I think they voted against distorting that kind of compassion into a belief that the goal should not be the care of the needy, but actually a redistribution of the earnings—the earnings of those who work to be shared with those whose only disability is a reluctance or refusal to work.

Now, we have an example of how far and how much this has been distorted in the philosophy of government today and I don't have to go too far afield to tell of an actual case within the last several months of a man who refused employ-ment. He was on welfare with his family and he was rein-stated on welfare because it was ruled that his extreme lazi-ness was an incurable ailment, and therefore he was entitled to welfare.

I think the people voted against the unnecessary harass-ment and regulation of every facet of our lives.

I think the people spoke of a hope to curb this prevalent philosophy. This philosophy is leading us toward a central-ization of authority in the national government, and away from the traditional concepts of local autonomy and individual freedom.

With terms like "guidelines," and "consensus," we face a controlled and planned economy, and sometimes, when you look at the efforts of the planners at every echelon of government, you wonder if they aren't a little like that fellow in the dark of the theatre who sits there winking at the chorus girls. He knows what he is doing, but nobody else does.

Well, this great ambitious corporation has grown. We can check and see—it's grown so much—we can check up and see that since the turn of the century, the gross national product of this nation has multiplied 33 times over, but the size of the federal government is 234 times greater than it was just at that time.

And there are new assaults being made on private initiative. They are on the bureaucratic drawing board in this era of instant legislation. And this is my hope that the last election meant that perhaps there is going to be a pause in this.

Here in California, we are embarked on, what I consider, a kind of an experiment . . . on a crusade to try to give back to the people the running of their own affairs.

We have a great problem of unemployment in California. We are 28 percent higher than the national average. We have terrible pockets of unemployment in certain areas, particularly among our minority groups. And we reaped perhaps the fruit of this more than a year and a half ago in the terrible uprisings in the Watts area of Los Angeles. Well, almost immediately, one man, a private industrialist here in this community—while the smoke was still in the air—marshalled businessmen and industrialists in a room like this and he said, "There is a challenge here that we can help meet. We can't do everything about it, but we do have a responsibility as businessmen. We are the only ones that can really, in the last analysis, give jobs."

And industry was mobilized by this man and this idea.

And today there are some 2,600 industrialists in the Los

Angeles area mobilized in an effort to provide work and they started just there in the curfew area in Los Angeles. And to date they have put more than 50 percent of the unemployed through job training and into jobs that already existed in private industry—productive jobs.

It's been a thrilling story and this man, Chad McClellen, has now accepted the responsibility that we have asked him to accept: to do this on a state-wide basis and put private industry throughout California to work to solve the problem, particularly in these great pockets of unemployment.

And yet, to show how far we have drifted in this philosophical approach, a Congressman, representing some of these very underprivileged people, has challenged this approach and said that it's the wrong way; that the only way to solve the problem is through a vast federal program of employment.

Well, I have to challenge him; I just don't believe that.

Congress is being asked to give the power to government to lay down the rules to shape the size and the printing on all packages . . . to authorize the Office of Consumer Research to investigate the productive capacity, and the distribution systems, and the quality and the degree of customer satisfaction, and to give government the power for annual and special-type investigations and reports and to demand such reports from business. Special reports. You realize that today the federal agencies receive five reports a year for every man, woman, child and baby in the United States, and the cost to industry for completing this paper work is more than the total dividends that are paid by all of our corporations to all of their stockholders in this country.

It is estimated that the small businessman, particularly, spends 35 percent of his time—his working time—making out government reports, forms and papers.

Lowell Mason, former anti-trust director, said in his book, *The Language of Dissent,* that in this country one sees a growing acceptance of the thesis that violation of the economic commands of the state is more dangerous to our national welfare than criminal offenses and, therefore, can be punished without due process . . . no resort to law, no chance to stand before a judge and jury—just by an administrative edict, punishment can be meted out.

Now what we have to recognize is that government does not produce freedom. People have a right to, or have to take, freedom from government and they must continue the struggle to keep it. I don't mean to infer with this that government is sitting there with some kind of devious plot or conspiracy in which they are aiming to enslave the people.

It just happens to be the thing the founding fathers were unique in recognizing—that this is the tendency of government; that we must recognize that all of us are stockholders and shareholders in government, from the first moment we pay the first penny of tax; that there can be no vacuum in this area of human relations; that if we do not make government our business, then government will proceed to run us. And this was never the intention in this great system of ours.

It's becoming clear that big government is not only incompetent to deliver many of its promises, but it also must resort to force and coercion under the guise of helping people. Let me just read you another quote.

"The doctrine of regulation—legislation by masterminds in whose judgment and will all the people may gladly and quietly acquiesce—has been too glaringly apparent in Washington. Were it possible to find masterminds so willing to decide unhesitatingly against their own personal interests, such a government might be to the interest of the country. But there are none such on the political horizon."

Now, what Neanderthal member of the right-wing conspiracy uttered that? It must have at least gone back to the days of McKinley. Well, actually, those words were spoken by Franklin Delano Roosevelt.

You know, it just makes us realize, I think, how close we are to running out of time. We are a little like the man that just had an examination by the doctor and very bravely, as he buttoned his shirt, said, "Tell me, Doc, I can take it; how much time have I got?" And the doctor said, "Let me put it to you this way—eat the best part of the chicken first."

Federal employees outnumber state employees in 30 of our 50 states including such a populous and big state as this. One out of six of the nation's work force is an employee of government. And you wonder where the breaking point is, if the government continues to expand. Are we supposed to stop when we get to one out of five? Or is it one out of four? Or one out of three?

When you stop to think about it—every five of us that is earning a living have an employee we are fully responsible for. We are paying the full rate for that sixth employee.

Well, what is the alternative? To sell the Post Office or cancel the highway program? A complete voluntarism that says no government involved at all?

Well there might be some purists who would recommend such, but I think it's far more sensible to recognize that there is another alternative to either the Great Society or such extreme laissez-faire.

I think it lies in remembering our own abilities . . . our own past accomplishments. The end of World War I, for instance, if we get into the field of relief or foreign aid. We saved millions of lives with an aid program, a foreign aid program, if you will, and it was mainly a voluntary effort on the part of the American people. With cooperation on the part of government, of course, but just think of this great program and what it accomplished and when the mission was accomplished, it disappeared, and we went our way until there was another great international catastrophe to call upon us—I think probably the next one was the great earthquake disaster in Tokyo—and again the American people rose up and did what had to be done.

The end of World War II . . . the Secretary of Commerce, Jesse Jones, was alarmed by the plans that he saw on the bureaucratic drawing boards in Washington. And realizing that there would be a tremendous pressure for government controls in the transition from war to peace, he called in the nation's business leaders and he told them, and he gave them the challenge and he said *you*—you tell us— to accept the leadership and evolve a plan that will make this transition without economic disruption or upheaval within our nation. And the top corporation leaders of this nation created a commission for economic development. Fifty-thousand businessmen nationwide, acting through 2,000 local committees, did the post-war planning and the prophets of economic doom who were spelling out what was going to happen to us in that transition were all wrong. The transition from war to peace was guided by independent effort, because one man saw a problem and knew the answer, and knew the answer lay in the great human resources of Americans and he knew that those human resources were far greater than the power of government.

The truth is, today we have to realize that this country, in its private sector has been fighting the most successful war on poverty the world has seen for the last 200 years.

Our West was built without an area redevelopment plan. They rebuilt after the fire and earthquake in San Francisco and they didn't wait for urban renewal to do it. We've done a great many things of this kind without declaring them disaster areas. If there were men in government who were capable of running the nation's business, the nation's business would have long since hired them away from government.

There are some who point to the present prosperity as proof that government intervention has been helpful to business. And they hold up this prosperity and they say: here is the answer. Well, I think it is no such thing. It is simply proof of the great virility of the free enterprise system that it could survive the nit-picking and the harassment and the meaningless regulations and regressive taxation at this time. But the virility is not and can't survive forever.

Remember the story of Gulliver: giant that he was for the little figures of Lilliput; eventually, when he relaxed too much he was enslaved, not with chains, but with just thread after thread after thread until eventually he was helpless and couldn't move at all.

I think we have to recognize that additional purchasing power, and hence prosperity, is not created by redistributing the earnings on hand, but by increasing production. I think we have to fall back on one of the most ancient of all economic laws: there's no such thing as free lunch.

And then, I think that, with this, we have a pattern to follow. We should restore to full power the contract that has guaranteed us the most limited and equitable government known to man. I am speaking of the Constitution. I think that we have to keep in mind that the purpose of the Bill of Rights was to forever put our right to control our own destiny beyond the reach of majority rule. It just does not follow that the majority is always right. In a lynch mob you have majority rule, and it doesn't make them right. Majority rule is a fine means in a democratic process for getting something achieved, only so long as we recognize that there is a set of ground rules that guarantees the individual certain rights that cannot be taken away from him even if he is out-voted by the rest of the people in the country.

Then, we recognize that there is an area—a legitimate area—for government control . . . for government regulation to make sure that, in our search for, or pursuit of happiness, we don't invade or interfere with someone else's right to the pursuit of happiness.

And, we recognize that government is at its best when it is kept close to the people. There are influential political minds in Washington who would eliminate state sovereignty as outmoded . . . who would make the states administrative districts of an all-powerful government.

I heard the story the other day of a teacher who boasted in the classroom that he would not require the learning of state capitals because he believed that, by the time the students got out of school, there wouldn't be such a thing. This would have come to pass if the administrative districts idea had jelled.

Well, states rights, I believe, are a built-in guarantee of freedom. As long as a citizen can vote with his feet—can move across a state border—the state is restrained in how far it can go in being tyrannical. It must always recognize that it must be able to keep the people within the state and hopefully to attract others to come to that state because of the freedom and opportunity it offers to them.

Every problem that besets us today—from dropouts to disease, from job retraining to student loans—is being solved somewhere in the country by a group of citizens who didn't wait for government . . . being solved right now. Perhaps we need better intercommunications—a system between us —an early warning system so that we can anticipate some of these problems and start to solve them at the private level so that when government turns its attention on us, with this problem as an excuse, we can say: sorry, we are already handling that situation.

There is a role for government—and, I believe, particularly at a state and local level—not as a substitute for the people, but as a leader in the development of a Creative Society, mobilizing the full resources of all the people. There are 18,000 business organizations in this country . . . 6,400 private foundations, worth about 15 billion dollars. There are about 320,000 churches, and 100,000 groups like the United Fund and the Community Chest.

Just to give you an idea of the powers that we, the people, have if we turn our attention to these things, let us look at that figure of just 320,000 churches. Now I don't mean that the church should take over the responsibility of employment. But, do you realize that if you pro-rated the actual hard-core unemployment in this country—heads of family seeking work—it comes out a little less than three per church? If you stop to think of that many people saying: here are three people we should help . . . three families we should get on their feet and find an answer to their problem —you begin to see the great power the people have.

There is more talent than government can possibly match . . . talent to fight a thousand wars on poverty.

This is no retreat into the past; this actually is taking a dream that we once had and bringing it forth within a twentieth-century model. I think we have had enough of 19th century rule of the many by the few, even if the few are supposed to be some kind of intellectual élite, who are more gifted than the rest of us.

We have come now to the time to implement real self-government. Problem one: the needy student. Well, how about expanding an organization that we already have in this country, started by private individuals, called The United Student Loan Fund or Student Aid Fund? This recognized the problem of needy students in getting an education. Banks lend money—legitimate commercial loans—to students to go to college, the loans not to be paid back until after graduation. Today there are some 65,000 recipients on more than 700 campuses, with more than 35 million dollars out in loans voluntarily underwritten by private citizens and business organizations in this country. This is a far better answer than a government, no interest, or low interest loan plan, because the government should not be in the lending business.

Slum clearance? look at the experiment going on in Harlem in New York . . . what the United States Gypsum Company has done with an experiment as to how they can rehabilitate slum dwellings. They are doing it at less than 50 percent of the cost of building a public housing unit and the family isn't even moved out as they restore ceilings and floors and walls and install new bathrooms and new kitchens. And, if they are successful in this and the word is spread, all of us in our urban problems can meet the real problem that exists, without dislocation, and without urban renewal, and at the same time, we will stimulate and not outcompete or destroy private enterprise. A Negro group on Long Island chipped in and bought a run-down hospital that had been closed, and now they have a going and efficient hospital in a neighborhood that needed it very badly.

This is what I take as the meaning of the election on November 8th, both here and across the nation. I suggest it to all of you, suggest it to all of you in your states, and, as businessmen, I suggest that you take another look. The businessman today is really old-fashioned who still believes that as a businessman he must have no participation in controversial things or in politics or government. If you go along with that philosophy, you are just feeding the crocodile, hoping that he will eat you last. And as we do this (and it should be done in every state), we are going to put the pressure on our Congressmen; we are going to demand of Congress that they give consideration—serious consideration—to legislation now pending in Washington that we want Washington —the great tax-eater—to earmark a certain percentage of the tax paid by the people of a state and give back that money or let it stay in the state with no strings attached. We know how to spend it best. And we will use it in our own state for our own state activities.

Senator George Murphy was the co-author of a bill in the last session. He has told me that he wants to introduce it again. It is a bill that gives parents sending children to college a tax credit—not a tax deduction—a tax credit for a part of the expense for sending their children to college as a write-off against their income tax.

If the government in Washington is truly concerned in helping higher education, and that concern is not tinged with a desire to dictate to higher education, then why should not the federal government set a figure say, a hundred dollars and allow every income taxpayer to submit to the government in lieu of that hundred dollar payment, or share of his income tax, a receipt indicating that he has contributed that hundred dollars to a university of his choice, whether it be public or private, and we would help solve some of the problems that are militating against higher education today.

The great home—the originator of freedom—ancient Athens in Greece . . . history tells us that when the freedom the Athenians wished for most was freedom from responsibility, Athens ceased to be free and was never free again.

We stand here on the only island of freedom that is left in the whole world. There is no place to flee to . . . no place to escape to. We defend freedom here or it is gone. There is no place for us to run, only to make a stand. And if we fail, I think we face telling our children, and our children's children, what it was we found more precious than freedom. Because I am sure that someday—if we fail in this—there will be a generation that will ask.

11. A SECRET BALLOT FOR UNIONS

I AM asking for legislation that will grant to union members the right of a secret ballot when voting on questions of internal union policy.

This is the first time any state has attempted to secure for union members the right to vote their consciences in those matters which affect the daily operations of the union and, therefore, have a vital effect on their personal lives.

For purposes of the legislation, these matters would be considered internal policy:

Seniority rules: rules of internal union discipline; the creation, administration or dissolution of union pension or welfare programs; whether expenditures not in the ordinary course of union business are proper; whether the union should engage in certain political activity; whether the union should strike or engage in picketing; whether to initiate collective bargaining negotiations; the terms desired to be included in a collective bargaining agreement; generally, any matter affecting the inner workings of a labor union and the

(*Submitted to the California Legislature April 6, 1967.*)

welfare of its members and not subject to the exclusive regulatory jurisdiction of federal labor laws and federal agencies.

This legislation is designed to give union members greater control over the affairs of their unions and to end minority control of some unions.

In addition, I am asking for further legislation aimed at eliminating financial conflicts of interest of officers and agents of labor organizations.

Under this legislation, union officers and agents would be prohibited from acquiring financial interests which interfere with the performance of their duties. The legislation also provides that unions account fully to their members for all assets and financial transactions.

Under the proposed legislation, both unions and employer organizations will file annual reports with the Director of Industrial Relations, showing financial transactions and the financial condition of the organization.

I am proposing that an advisory council of three members be appointed by the Governor to inform the Governor and the Legislature concerning the operation, administration and enforcement of the provisions of the act. The board also will make recommendations for the improvement or revision of the act.

12. OUR POLLUTED AIR, WATER AND LAND

THERE is immediate need for a California Waste Management Program designed to end the pollution of our air, water and land. Such pollution is a major threat to public health, economic growth and the quality of our California environment.

Specific legislation is directed at making California the first state in the nation to adopt a comprehensive threefold approach to the very critical problems of pollution.

There are serious gaps in state policy and a piecemeal fragmentation of governmental units which now characterize the waste management field. There is an absence of state policy goals aimed at improving the quality of our environment. And there is little ability now to control the major sources of pollution.

We must adopt a systematic program of action in this field. To meet this need, we are proposing a policy that would:

1—Reorganize and consolidate the existing fragmented government systems by establishing single state governmen-

(*A statement on California's Waste Management Program, Feb. 16, 1967.*)

tal units in the fields of air resources, water resources and solid waste disposal. I cannot emphasize too strongly, however, that this consolidation must preserve local responsibilities.

2—Establish tough anti-pollution standards, especially in the field of air pollution.

3—Recognize that the related problems of air pollution, water pollution and solid waste disposal are part of the general problem of protecting the quality of California's environment.

I am, therefore, recommending legislation establishing a single Air Resources Board. This Board would have jurisdiction not only in the field of motor vehicle emissions now covered by law, but also over air pollution from stationary sources such as open burning, burning dumps and industrial-commercial operations.

This legislation would authorize the Air Resources Board to adopt standards governing the composition of diesel and other motor fuels and would establish a state-wide air monitoring system. Educational efforts on the very serious problems of air pollution would be stepped up.

In addition, a major requirement in the field of air pollution should be a provision that vehicle emission devices be designed to meet 1970 standards. This would give the automotive industry and others a three-year period in which to develop and improve emission devices that would meet a definite and minimum goal set for 1970.

Until now, limited responsibilities for air pollution control have been vested at all levels of government. The result has been an inability to develop a program that considers the total air pollution burden on the air resources throughout a region.

Legislation is also needed to establish a single unit of state government for liquid waste management. Responsibility for water quality control, according to a report by the "Little Hoover Commission," is diffused among the State Water

Quality Control Board, nine Regional Water Quality Control Boards, the Department of Water Resources, the Department of Public Health, the Department of Fish and Game and waste discharges under self-monitoring arrangements.

The Assembly Water Committee, headed by Assemblyman Carley Porter, has recommended merging the State Water Rights and Water Quality Control Boards and I look with approval on this measure.

Finally, legislation should be enacted which would designate responsibility within the Department of Public Health for developing solid waste management policies and standards and for undertaking research and development. In this field of refuse and sanitation, no state agency now has the statutory responsibility for planning and development of standards.

I would also suggest that legislation creating a California Waste Management Act of 1967 be enacted, establishing an Environmental Quality Board to provide a unified approach to solving the problems of pollution control and improving the quality of our environment.

Such a Board would resolve policy conflicts between air, water and solid waste disposal agencies and would make recommendations to the Governor and the Legislature to prevent pollution. Representatives on the Board might include those from the agencies in the water, air and solid waste fields. Other members could be representatives on the League of Cities, County Supervisors Assn., State Planning Office, the Legislature and the state Chamber of Commerce.

Such a Board, involving all segments of the population, would allow the needed flexibility necessary to implement pollution controls on the local and regional levels.

What I have outlined will have a very limited immediate cost but will result in significantly improved programs for making our environment livable. As state responsibility broadens, and this unique approach results in a cleaner and better California, costs will increase. But federal grants can be expected in the future to finance this tremendously improved and vitally important program.

This "Waste Management Program" provides California with the opportunity to pioneer among all the states of this nation in the waste management field.

California cannot afford to lose its three most valuable resources. If the air cannot be breathed, if the water is unfit for drinking, if the land is despoiled by our own refuse, we will have nothing. If we permit the befouling of our air, our water, our land, we shortly will be unable to live in this great state.

I am thoroughly convinced that we must act—and act now. At best, our current efforts are barely keeping even with the problem. Much greater effort must be put forth. Enactment of this program is the first step toward a brighter future.

13. CONSERVATION, RECREATION
AND TOMORROW

I⊤ is part of the conservative philosophy to preserve the best of our heritage—including our natural resources. But the conservative philosophy also demands that the best use be made of those resources we preserve.

We recognize that what we are doing today is not enough. We must prepare for tomorrow—to make parks and recreation even more readily available to the increasing millions of Californians and others who need to share and who have a right to share in all that California has to offer.

We must examine and plan for our environment and how it properly relates to the economic progress of our state.

Let me point out that about half of California is federally owned. Most of that land is mountain and forest land in the Sierras. We are working to persuade the federal government to make more of these lands available for recreational development and use.

We think that it is possible to evolve an integrated program

(From a speech to the California and Pacific Southwest Recreation and Park Conference.)

with the federal government, letting it concentrate on the mountains while we concentrate on providing recreation along the coast, in the desert and in the interior valleys.

A special technical task force made up of planners, ecologists, landscape architects and engineers is now studying the problem of locating an all-year-round road on the west side of Lake Tahoe. This will be done by environmental planning so that the unique resources of the area will be protected, at the same time providing for the transportation of people and things. Quality and creativity are being emphasized in all of our planning efforts.

As part of that emphasis, we intend to take a strong look at possible ways of bringing parks to people. Everybody does not have the time or the money to travel to the desert or to the mountains or to the wilderness areas.

We think there should be a way to give our city and slum dwellers the advantages of parks on as nearly a daily basis as they wish. The quiet and tranquility of the great city parks such as Central Park and Griffith Park can do much for modern man in today's hurried and harried living.

And, the small neighborhood parks can go a long way toward keeping our boys and girls off the streets and channeling their energies into worthwhile activities. As our cities and urban areas continue to grow, the need for new parks grows greater and the strain on existing facilities mounts ever higher.

Thus, the challenge to the Department of Parks and Recreation is clear. Its responsibility is not only to protect the environmental quality of California, but also to provide for the recreational needs of her people. In reorganizing the department, it was not our intention to give greater emphasis to these recreational needs than to preservation of the natural resources of this state, but rather to provide an organizational structure that would recognize not only the preservation and conservation responsibilities that the department holds, but also to accept the challenge of constructively providing for the leisure-time demands of our citizens.

We recognize also that good conservation practices go beyond merely preserving what we have left. We must also be in the business of reclamation, as well as that of protection. We must not only protect our rivers, lakes, bays and beaches from pollution; we must reclaim and purify those that have been polluted. And, we must do the same for our air.

Referring to Tahoe—that unique beauty spot we share with our neighbor state, Nevada—years of frustration were ended with the establishment by our legislature of the Tahoe Regional Planning Agency which will move toward protection of the unparalleled beauty of the area while insuring balanced recreational and economic development there. In the best spirit of neighborliness and cooperation, the Governor and the legislature of Nevada enacted similar Tahoe legislation so that both states can move forward together.

We must come to grips now with the total environmental needs of people and their enjoyment of life as it pertains to the quality of air and water and its availability; to the proper protection and use of the land and the rivers and streams, lest there be none; to the creation of a balanced transportation system, lest we be overwhelmed by autos and freeways, aircraft and airports, rails and terminals—all gobbling up the land, without plan or coordination. We must study noise and its effects on people, the potential of thermal and nuclear pollution, and we must have adequate parks, recreation areas and space, and peace and quiet for people and living.

It is possible that we will see a Redwood National Park in the next year or two. And this is well and good. But let me emphasize that we do not need a national park to protect our redwoods. California has already done that. Most of the remaining virgin growths of the redwoods are already protected in state parks. And let me point out that any national park, to be meaningful, will have to encompass at least two state parks. Desirable as a Redwood National Park may be, we are insisting that at the same time the economy of our Northern California timber areas be protected. And we are also insisting that the federal government, in return for our redwoods, give us beach and mountain lands that can be developed by California into useable recreational areas.

We recognize that the future is in the hands of our youth. The youth of today will either be the protectors or the destroyers of our land.

We are concerned with the problems of coastal development and conservation. We know too little of the enormous values for mankind of proper understanding and use of our coastal resources and the sea. But we are going to know more.

Legislation has already been enacted creating the Middle Fork of the Feather River as a wild river. This fifty-mile stretch of nature will provide a primitive area where man can enjoy the outdoors as it was before he arrived.

California is also progressing in the area of open space protection as it relates to land usage and the tax base. Few realize the extent to which green grass is giving way to blacktop, but the threat is real and serious. Open land in Southern California is being converted to urban uses at a rate of 70 square miles per year. You can get some idea of what that means if you think of the city of San Francisco occupying only 44 square miles.

Legislation was passed last year to provide tax relief for agricultural lands that remain as open space.

Though we are moving in these many specific areas of resource protection, all of it and more must come together to produce an environment which will provide for the people of this state a healthy and exciting place to live, next year, ten years hence and in the year 2000—just 32 years from now when as many as 50 million people may live in our state.

It is essential that they understand the value of our land,

streams and countryside; protect it from litter and degradation; leave it unsullied for future generations because if it is destroyed, it is lost forever. We are determined not to let that happen.

14. LET'S USE THE OCEAN

OCEANOGRAPHY has important long-range implications to the U.S. and to the world, and especially to those areas bordering on the seas.

There is little argument that sea water, sea life, both plant and animal, and sea bottoms contain the potential vastly to expand our food production, our mineral production and in general the world's wealth.

And, of course, advancing technology makes it increasingly apparent that the oceans in the not too distant future can supply major amounts of potable water to our coastal areas.

Here in California where we have large water-short areas we are vitally interested in desalinization concepts and processes.

We have watched with deep interest the progress made in recent years in bringing down the price of desalinated water to the point where today it is becoming feasible to use it in our city water systems.

In fact, if the off-shore plant which will function from a

(Address at Marine Technology Society banquet, San Diego.)

man-made island off Huntington Beach operates as expected when completed in 1972, we will finally have what is pretty close to a major breakthrough in the production of fresh water—20 cents for every thousand gallons, and 150 million gallons of water a day.

Since water is of such tremendous importance to California let me digress just a moment to mention that sea water is only one of several possibilities for furnishing fresh water to our growing millions.

Ocean-oriented engineers have also talked of bringing water to Southern California in huge pipes laid off our coast either from the mouth of the Columbia River or perhaps from the mouth of the Feather.

Many experts believe this is possible but certainly much more research and engineering study must be done before we can say it is practical. And of course at this end it must meet one of the same obstacles that desalinated water faces. It must be pumped from sea level to those areas needing it.

If such a project is otherwise practical this one obstacle is not insurmountable. Our great California water project will pump water over the Techapis and into our arid areas south of the mountains. And, of course, water from the Colorado is pumped in also.

A third area is that of reclaimed water. A good share of our water is used only once and then is carried off to sea. While the subject of reclaiming water may not be a proper one for an oceanographic meeting, certainly the development of ways and means to reclaim waste water is vital to our future. There are indications that this not only might be the cheapest solution to our long-range water problems, but it is also evident that a successful solution would minimize' the need for further importation of water.

Sometimes I wonder where we might be today had we had the vision to look at the sea and at water reclamation methods 30 or 40 years ago and had spent on these projects just a fraction of the amount we have spent in bringing water in from the Colorado and down from the north.

But the problem of fresh water is only one of the many problems facing California, the Pacific coast and much of the world today that oceanographers can help solve.

The excitement and titillation of oceanography is the picture of the futuristic submarine and the man in the diving suit, it is the talk of distilling gold and other precious minerals from sea water, it is the vision of supplying world food needs from the sea.

But much of this futuristic world is already here. In fact, magnesium, bromine and potassium have been extracted commercially from the waters off America and one of California's major salt suppliers extracts its product solely from the sea.

New-type submarines and diving bells with arm-like mechanical claws are already exploring the oceans at great depths.

And aquaculture is becoming increasingly important in Japan including establishment of an oyster program in California which now produces 7,610 million pounds annually. Small-scale projects also are underway in the United States, but studies indicate there is much to be done in this area before sea-farming as differentiated from commercial fishing becomes an important source of the world's food.

While exploring the possibilities the ocean offers in new or exotic fields, we should not overlook these areas in which man has used the ocean since time immemorial—fishing and commerce.

Both of these fields are of vital importance to California, to the West Coast and to the entire Pacific basin.

Some of you may not be aware of it but for years San Pedro has been one of the world's major fishing ports and San Diego has been not far behind.

But irresponsible commercial fishing, primarily by other

nations has cut into the world's supply of edible fish such as tuna. Both a research program and international agreements are needed to develop and control means of levelling out catches and insuring sustained yields of commercial fishes.

Already great strides have been made in converting some species of fish, once thought of as non-edible, into fish flour, but more can be done in this area. A 1964 study found that the amount of animal protein needed for the entire world could be obtained by a mere 30 percent increase in the world fish catch, provided of course the means of distribution could be found.

But distribution of goods and things by sea is an area where we in the U.S. are falling badly behind.

California harbors, for instance, cannot handle the super-ships now being built. Japan has one ship with a capacity of 150,000 tons and a draft of 66 feet, seven inches. San Francisco's main ship channel has a depth of just 45 feet.

It is obvious that either harbors must be improved or new and economical methods of off-shore loading must be found.

Largely because of economic conditions the U.S. in general has fallen farther and farther behind the rest of the world in shipbuilding and in cargo hauling.

California shipyards now operate at less than half their capacity. America's share of ocean-going cargo is constantly decreasing.

Here are areas where American ingenuity, inventiveness and initiative can change the picture, especially if government, industry and labor are willing to cooperate with each other.

In California we hope and plan to have a major hand in that change. Just as we also plan to take a major part in studying the ocean itself, its effect on climate, and its resources.

We think California, with its 1200-mile coastline, with its research and technology-oriented industries and universities, with its great numbers of qualified and brilliant engineers and scientists, should lead the way.

California has much to gain from a determined effort to orient itself toward the ocean.

Our rapidly growing population needs not only water, it also needs jobs. Heretofore we have been a state oriented to agriculture and defense industries. Agriculture must continue to play a major role in the state's economy, and defense will also be of vast importance in the foreseeable future.

But we should not depend on federal funds as the basis for an industrial economy and advancing technologies will continue to cut down the numbers employed in agri-business while at the same time increasing production.

Therefore, California must turn in other directions to prepare for the future. One direction is west and that way lies the ocean.

Industry has become more and more aware of the ocean potential. Lockheed Board Chairman, Daniel L. Haughton, for instance, has called for the aerospace and petroleum industries "to join forces in exploration and development of the Continental Shelves."

Certainly, similar arrangements might mutually benefit many of our industries.

This state administration feels it has an obligation to lead the way. Not to tell business and industry and research what must be done, not to dip deep into the taxpayers' pocket to provide a kind of subsidized approach, but instead to encourage, to work with and to provide the kind of governmental climate in which the many faces of oceanography can become meaningful, can spur the economy and increase our progress.

We have already begun.

I have appointed an expert in the field, Col. T. R. Gillenwaters, as a special advisor to lead this effort.

We have reactivated the Governor's Advisory Commission

on Ocean Resources. This is made up of top men in the oceanographic field.

This Commission, called GACOR, already has recom mended creation of an inter-agency council for ocean re sources. If our studies find this practical, such a council could well be the forerunner to a state office of Marine Resources.

Such an office could correlate interstate activities as well as coordinating federal-state activities and above all, offering support and help to the independent sector which, after all, must provide the main thrust if California is to develop as a major sea state.

But we envision looking beyond the borders of California, also. A sea-oriented state must look to others with the same interests and the same problems.

As soon as it can be conveniently done, I hope to meet with my fellow Governors from Washington, Oregon, Hawaii and Alaska to discuss the concept of a Pacific Basin Com munity.

Such a community eventually could look toward working with our neighbors of both the north and south, Canada and Mexico, in solving mutual problems, exchanging ideas and information.

A Pacific Basin Community of states could activate broad programs involving cooperation among the states, the federal government and the independent sector.

These programs could be as wide and varied as the field of oceanography itself.

These would include research into utilization of ocean re sources, resolution of maritime legal questions; tax incen tives; review and analysis of all related federal and state legis lation, ways of improving maritime trade, fisheries research and development; ways and means of expanding mineral and oil exploration along the Continental Shelf, desalinization; pollution control in tidal and bay areas; improved weather and tide forecasting, and expanded recreational facilities.

In an era of spending billions for space exploration and

many billions more for defense and for social experiments, the oceans have been largely overlooked except as how they affect the military.

The time has come to end the oversight, the time has come to look to the seas as we build for the future.

15. THE RIGHT OF THE PEOPLE TO KNOW

SOMETIMES it has seemed to me that newspapers let their policies get in the way of objectivity and accuracy. Here in California, for example, we have an axis that begins in Los Angeles in the morning and ends up in Sacramento in the afternoon. And it sometimes seems, that news, as they print it, is what they wish it were instead of what it actually is. Now, I don't want to give the impression that this kind of reporting could actually influence anyone, but after reading their accounts of what I'm supposed to be doing, I did go out the other day and sign a recall petition and I was the subject of the recall.

A good reporter in the field of politics must depend on the usually "reliable" source, and as a result, he sometimes gets blamed when the "reliable" source turns out unreliable. One such story made its appearance recently regarding our administration. It was headlined as an inside story, and it was a great story. It just didn't happen to be true.

(*Excerpts from a speech to United Press International Editors, San Francisco.*)

There is, too, the case of a syndicated columnist who must have gotten her story after a visit to Haight-Ashbury. She gave a first-hand account of my meeting with Governor Johnson of Mississippi—my questions to him, and his advice to me, on how to run for president in the southern states. For this kind of story, there was no excuse, and I demanded a retraction even though I've lived my life believing that retractions never appear in large print and if anyone notices them at all, they only give the reader an appetite to go back and read the original story he missed in the first place. I've never met Governor Johnson. And, I have a wire in which Governor Johnson says he never met me.

In actuality, I will be the staunchest defender of a reporter's right to speak his piece. He and I have one thing in common—we are custodians of a public trust. All of us who hold public office, of course, are. And the public trust of the press is to see that it keeps the people informed. And I think, by and large, down through the years, it has done just that. But someplace along the line, there has been a loosening . . . liberties are being taken . . . agencies of government at every level are seeking to perform their services more and more with less and less attention to the right of the people to know. And by the same token, there have been those in the profession who have violated their trust, their responsibility to keep the people informed.

Let me seriously give just one example and leave it to public judgment whether someone has not betrayed a trust.

Recently, one of the wire services sent a story datelined Da Nang, Vietnam. The story read, "A marine helicopter pilot saw 50 Viet Cong torturing four wounded American soldiers on the beach below." One of the most respected of the major eastern newspapers ran that story and it read, "A United States Marine helicopter pilot, answering the radioed call for help, saw 50 Viet Cong holding four wounded American soldiers on the beach below."

The wire service story went on to say that it took 20 minutes of scrambling across a soft South China Sea beach to drag three of the Americans aboard, while a South Vietnamese Air Force helicopter picked up the body of the fourth whose throat had been cut. The paper ran that section of the story, changing the last sentence, however, to simply read that the other Air Force helicopter picked up the body of the fourth. The wire service story quoted one of the officers aboard the helicopter as saying it looked as if they wanted to mutilate them, strip them and leave them in a line for display. The newspaper ran the story "all four had been wounded in the gunfight before the helicopter arrived."

Perhaps one can argue the editorial right to not be too brutal in the telling of the story, not to mention the slitting of a throat by the enemy. But one has to ask, is there also not a right when the government's policy is being assailed, of the people to get the factual information about the enemy we are fighting and the tactics being used.

When press associations or journalists' clubs meet, I would hope there would be a continuing re-evaluation, not only of news gathering, and news gatherers, but also of the place of interpretive reporting in news-writing and the value, if any, of the political gossip columnists and rumor-mongers.

I am not an expert in the newspaper business, but now that I have become increasingly a subject of its stories and columns and speculation, I am concerned, indeed concerned, about the responsibility of both the press and those of us in the business of government to resist the temptation to influence public thinking by keeping from the public the facts, whether pleasant or unpleasant, and to make sure they *are* facts.

16. THE PERILS OF GOVERNMENT-SPONSORED HIGHER EDUCATION

CALTECH's plans for the future are exciting—exciting to me as a citizen and a father, and as the governor of the most technological state in the union, who properly should from time to time take stock of this state's great resources—and the California Institute of Technology is a unique resource, one of California's most valuable. It is easy to see that what Caltech is setting out to accomplish in the period ahead is important not just to southern California and not alone even to the whole state of California. It will benefit the nation and the world. Caltech long ago ceased to be merely a local asset. The results of its research and education have accelerated the flow of new science and technology and their utilization throughout the globe.

I should like to discuss some thoughts about the importance of higher education and of science and technology, about the matching to technical change of appropriate social development and maturity, about the using of advancing science and technology to the fullest, achieving the promises

(From a speech at California Institute of Technology.)

that are ahead and minimizing—if not eliminating—the negatives resulting from the high rate of scientific and technological change. I should like to raise the question of how our handling of expanding science and technology affects the individual, his independence, his creativity, his freedom. And I should like to comment on the role, as I see it, of the private university and colleges, and its relation to the growing influence of government on all aspects of our lives, including science and technology.

It is easy to find on the record what Caltech's engineers have done for the here and now. Their research in aeronautics has influenced the design and performance of all commercial and military aircraft—a direct contribution to southern California's pre-eminence in the aviation industry.

Their hydraulics engineers have established the technological basis for pumping and channeling Colorado River water to our metropolitan water district.

Their electrical engineers have provided the technological foundation for the system and equipment that enabled the Southern California Edison Company to bring hydroelectric power from the Colorado River, across the mountains, to this region.

Caltech's studies of underground temperatures and pressures have pointed the way toward improvements in drilling efficiency which, in turn, have vastly increased southern California's petroleum production.

Its earthquake engineering program is directly responsible for the specifications that have at last made it safe to construct tall buildings in the "quake-prone" areas.

And its great Jet Propulsion Laboratory has made history, and will make more, in the exploration of space. It produced America's first satellite, Explorer I. It produced the first instrument to probe the space near Venus, the first close-up photographs of the planet Mars. And it produced the first soft landing of instruments and the first excavation on the moon.

These examples of Caltech's superb accomplishments of

the past speak for themselves, but they tell us something else as well: science and technology represent together a powerful force engaged in changing our world. Now, this adds problems as well as benefits; and one problem is the interaction of advancing science and technology upon our society—more specifically, the real dangers to freedom of the individual in the coming technological society; dangers, that is, if we don't arrange for our society to preserve these freedoms, if we are not intent on advancing mankind as well as his technology. We need more science because it can solve problems and be used to elevate man, but we need to match science with skill in applying it for the good of society.

A college is not just a vending machine dispensing packaged knowledge; it must impart wisdom. I understand that Caltech is planning a major program on the relation of science to society, starting with a fundamental attack on the distinction between living and inanimate matter, and building up from that eventually to understanding people. It is well known that Caltech has already cracked the genetic code and is deep into the understanding of the molecules that are indispensable to life processes. My staff, in doing homework, further tells me it was the recognition by Caltech's biologists of the underlying phenomena that has led to much of the progress in tissue and organ transplants. So it is reasonable for us laymen to take seriously what we now hear said by Caltech scientists—that we are approaching a new era in the control and cure of disease, in the increase of longevity, and even that we are soon to arrive at a capability to influence the human species.

I believe this. I accept its being only a question of time until these developments come. The *potential* good for all mankind will be enormous. But I cannot help reflecting that such developments can be thwarted, neutralized, even turned to evil if we do not match them with appropriate social advance. How ludicrous, but nevertheless realistic, it is that here our civilization's scientists are learning how to increase man's life span and finding ways to affect the genes to improve man, and are doing both at a faster rate than the same civilization is learning how to avoid the population explosion that threatens the ruination of our civilization.

Caltech is also planning to continue the search for answers on what matter and energy really consist of, down to understanding even more fundamentally than is now possible the makeup of the tiniest particles of matter—from which I am again ready to believe we shall have under man's control in the coming decades even greater amounts of energy to unleash than we now have. We shall be able to move mountains, change the earth's terrain and the weather above it, desalt the oceans if we choose. But this same society that makes such scientific advance has not yet learned how to live with itself so as to preclude the use of such energy for society's destruction.

I notice that in Caltech's plans there is the further scrutiny of mysterious radiation from outer space. Perhaps the secret will be found of those things known as "Quasars," which are not stars but sometimes look like stars, and that produce so much more energy than we have any way of explaining today. In some of that radiation from outer space the answer may be found to the question as to whether or not there is intelligent life on some distant planet or some remote star. But I cannot help saying that I am equally interested upon occasion in the question: do we have intelligent life on earth? Our present space program did not result because a mature society properly, deliberately, imaginatively pitted the potential benefits against our available resources to attain the best match. Rather, it has resulted in major part from reactions rather than plans—reactions to the unexpected prestige accomplishments of another nation.

There is, in fact, room for questioning whether our space program today has the right balance among space developments for national security, which deserve the highest priority; scientific space exploration which undoubtedly will in time bring us profitable new discoveries; and space developments that speed economic growth in the short term, such as communications satellites.

The Caltech program also includes major advances in the use of electronics to extend man's intellect, to provide the technological fundamentals for vast memory and for information processing at tremendous rates and with pervasive capacity and availability. This will lead to our ability to automate and enhance greatly the material operations of our society. Here, again, we had better match such technological advance with social understanding and action so as to have not a robot society run by computers, but one where we put all of this advanced science and technology to work as new tools for man so he can attain a higher life of greater personal freedom, versatility, skill, incentive, and creativity.

After all, if scientists are going to teach us how we can control the genes to alter the species and to make it possible for young couples to choose that their child be 10 percent like Einstein, 10 percent like father, 10 percent like mother, and 70 percent like Cary Grant, if you will, then let us try to evolve a pattern of society that permits these decisions to be made by the parents—not by some central computer in the government that will figure out what kinds of kids are best for all of us to have and then order up the right multi-digit formula for the genes so the mothers will give birth only to docile, standardized automatons in a thoroughly regimented society.

Yes, there must be public concern about the possible imbalance—the mismatch—of scientific and social advance. So to me the most exciting thing of all is Caltech's future plan to apply the strength of the scientific approach to the acceleration of the human side, the social side of life. I am informed that Caltech is acutely aware of the lack of harmony between scientific progress and social progress, and is setting about to contribute to the creation of a better tie.

The program starts with fundamentals. Human behavior

is a function of the human brain. Very little is known about this miraculous instrument, but surely something useful can be learned if it is studied at the level of molecular biology, as Caltech plans to do. And because the workings of the brain and the workings of a complex computer offer some potential similarities and interesting contrasts, I understand that Caltech has its biologists and its engineers closely allied in this endeavor. Their goal is no less than a practical understanding of the mechanics of thought, memory, consciousness, and emotion—and thus an understanding of the behavior of the human animal.

Thus, Caltech, in many ways, is unique. But it shares with other institutions of higher learning and research, whether state-sponsored or privately-supported, the need for large funds. And here there are problems, several different kinds of problems, facing all institutions of higher learning. To begin with, higher education has to be looked upon as an investment. Both basic research and higher education, properly conceived and directed, benefit the whole society. Some of the benefits take years for realization and even for evaluation. Many citizens, many individuals of independent means, lack the patience and the foresight to appreciate the investment aspect of higher education. In any case, the competition for funds for other necessary aspects of life makes it difficult to ensure the ready availability of sponsorship to the degree both desirable and, certainly in the long run, justifiable both for higher education and research.

How do we ensure that this kind of asset, Caltech, and the approach it uses of uninhibited, individualistic effort to understand the fundamentals of nature on behalf of mankind, will continue to receive sponsorship in this day and age? Such sponsorship, the backing of Caltech and of higher education in general, must come in the end from the community. But the community may be looked upon as consisting of two categories. One of them is people organized as a government to serve the rest of the people.

Our government agencies on all levels—local, state, and federal—are to varying degrees involved in scientific research. At the local level, it is mostly a matter of operating schools that help children learn something about science. At the state level, it involves the establishing and financing of universities and colleges engaged in research. At the federal level, it is an enormous and very deep commitment.

I must make my position very clear. The federal government's participation in scientific and engineering research is to an extent inevitable and desirable. The pace, risk, and magnitude of some of today's problems—especially in the area of defense—demand that the federal government underwrite—and control—many parts of the total research effort. But let us plan to watch this federal government involvement.

While the interaction between scientific research and the community promises many good things, it also is surrounded by dangers. There are literally hundreds of so-called "private" colleges and universities in this country, including some of our finest, that are so heavily dependent—especially in the fields of science and engineering—upon the federal government as to be in danger of losing what matters most—their identity, their individuality, their integrity, their independence.

I sympathize with students when they resent becoming a set of digits on a punched card without individuality. However, I believe there is something even worse; that is, direction, decision-making, and control of research and teaching coming not from individually brilliant, independent minds, but out of a huge, centralized government bureaucracy. I do not mean that the colleges so controlled are likely to be victims of a plot. I am not talking about Democrats or Republicans. But I *am* talking about politics in the sense that a political administration can generate bureaucracy—and any bureaucracy can be a threat to honest inquiry, and honest inquiry is the heart and soul of scientific research.

The federal government now spends about $4 billion a year on college campuses, and half of this goes for government-desired research. I will not pretend that I can evaluate all aspects of this outlay. I have no doubt that much of it can be justified. But I think all of us should ponder the figure and its impact upon the many private colleges and universities whose backs are now, financially, to the wall. They will crave this kind of support. Very likely, they will seek it. But how many of them can accept it and still hold on to their integrity?

A precious few, such as Caltech, may be able to do it indefinitely. I understand that, although Caltech today gets a substantial fraction of its operating funds from the federal budget, the federal part is for extraordinary services rendered. It is not really money that Caltech today depends upon to pursue its very special, independent goals. But it *is money* and, considering the desperate need for money among even the most staunch and dedicated seats of learning, it is not going to be despised or lightly rejected.

The second category of the community as a sponsor for higher education and scientific research is the private community—independent individuals, corporations, and foundations.

The part of the community represented by the federal government aggressively does its part. The question is whether the private part of the community—individuals, corporations, and foundations—does *its* part. I have my doubts. I fear that too many who would like to and could do something about guaranteeing independence from government control over research, who are in a position to make generous private grants, don't get around to it. They may even use their time and energy decrying the steady, increasing encroachment of government control upon more and more facets of our lives, while at the same time allowing, by default, the federal government to do exactly that.

The independent, private sector of the community can do

more than make financial contributions to private universities to guarantee their existence. This sector can also press for new ideas for the federal government's action to aid in providing superior incentives for private giving. For instance, tax credits for certain college expenses, better tax incentives for sponsorship of basic research in the colleges and universities.

Nor does the support of the private universities by the private sector imply any less support for the important state-supported universities and colleges. I am a devout believer in the benefits of competition, even in higher education. In California, where we have both high grade state institutions and private ones, strong support for both will work to the advantage of quality in both.

17. WHAT IS ACADEMIC FREEDOM?

IF ALL the problems of finance could be solved tomorrow, there would still be cause for concern about the place of higher education in contemporary America.

What is our definition of academic freedom?

Those who teach, define it as the right to teach as they see fit without interference from administrators and certainly not from those who hold the public purse strings or who fill the public purse.

But those who pay for the education, students and taxpayers, also have a definition of academic freedom: their freedom to have some say in what they get for their money.

Those holding public office try to interpret the will of the people and pass it on to the university administration, conscious always that they must not appear to be exerting political control over education. Equally uncomfortable are the administrators who must interpret the educators' viewpoint to the crass politicians and vice versa—they can be likened to a

(*From a speech to the California Federation of Republican Women, San Francisco.*)

prisoner in front of a cellophane wall being shouted at by both sides.

And the truth is—all the claims are legitimate and must be reconciled within a framework of mutual understanding and compromise.

The dictionary defines education as "the impartation or acquisition of knowledge, skill, or the development of character as by study or discipline."

The taxpayer is wrong who ignores the great increase in things we know—knowledge acquired since he was in school —and who demands "no new-fangled courses. What was good enough then is good enough now."

But so is the student wrong who would eliminate all required courses and grades—who would make education a kind of four-year smorgasbord in which he would be the sole judge of how far and fast he ran in pursuit of knowledge.

And that educator is wrong who denies there are any absolutes—who sees no black and white of right or wrong, but just shades of gray in a world where discipline of any kind is an intolerable interference with the right of the individual. He rebels at the old-fashioned idea of "loco parentis" and claims he is there to impart knowledge, not to substitute for absentee parents. But he cannot escape a responsibility for the students' development of character and maturity.

Strangely and illogically, this is very often the same educator who interprets his academic freedom as the right to indoctrinate students with his view of things. Woe to the student who challenges his interpretation of history, or who questions the economic theory given as proven formula in what is, at best, a very inexact science.

One thing we should all be agreed on is the university's obligation to teach, not indoctrinate.

These institutions were created, and are presently maintained, to insure perpetuation of a social structure—a nation, if you will.

Now don't put a narrow interpretation on this as some will,

and translate "social structure" into "status quo" or "social order" or "preserve the aristocracy; keep the little bananas from becoming top banana."

Our nation is founded on a concern for the individual and his right to fulfillment, and this should be the preoccupation of our schools and colleges.

The graduate should go forth, literally starting on a lifetime of learning and growing and creativity that will in turn bring growth and innovation to our society.

And the truth is—never in history has there been such a need for men and women of wisdom and courage—wisdom to absorb the knowledge of the past and plan its application to the present and future, and courage to make the hard decisions.

At Stanford University in 1906 William James said, "The wealth of a nation consists more than in anything else in the number of superior men that it harbors."

At the risk of great oversimplification may I suggest that the great ideological split dividing us on the world scene and here within our own borders has to do with the place of the individual.

Acceptance is given more and more to the concept of lifting men by mass movements and collective action, in spite of the fact that history is strangely barren of any record of advances made in this manner. By contrast, the road from the swamp to the stars is studded with the names of individuals who achieved fulfillment and lifted mankind another rung.

It is time we realized what we mean by "equality" and being "born equal."

We are equal before God and the law, and our society guarantees that no acquisition of property during our lifetime, nor achievement, no matter how exemplary, should give us more protection than those of less prestige, nor should it exempt us from any of the restrictions and punishments imposed by law.

But let there be no misunderstanding about the right of

man to achieve above the capacity of his fellows. The world is richer because of a Shakespeare and a Tennyson, a Beethoven and a Brahms. Certainly major league baseball would not be improved by letting every citizen who wanted to, have a turn at playing Willie Mays' position.

We live (even many so-called poor) at a level above the wildest dreams of the kings of one hundred years ago—because some individual thought of a horseless carriage, an ice box and later a refrigerator, or machinery that lifted burdens from our backs.

Why did so much of this develop so far and fast in America? Other countries are blessed with natural resources and equable climate—yes, and energetic and talented people.

But here, to a degree unequalled any place in the world, we unleashed the individual genius of man, recognized his inherent dignity, and rewarded him commensurate with his ability and achievement.

The student generation is being wooed by many who charge that this way we have known is inadequate to meet the challenges of our times. They point to the unsolved problems of poverty and prejudice as proof of the system's failure.

But students have a duty to find out if the failure is one of system—or is it the inadequacy of human nature?

They should also inquire if those who would replace the system have anything to offer in exchange other than untried theory packaged as Utopia. It sometimes seems strange that what is so often described as the brave new world of the future must be upheld by the collectivist philosophy of nineteenth-century theorists like Rousseau, Fourier and Marx.

Young people today live their entire lives in a governmental framework tending ever more toward the welfare state and centralism. We still have government of the people, by the people and for the people, but there seems to be a lot more of "for" the people and less "of" and "by." This is justified on the claim that society has grown so complex we can no longer afford too much individual freedom.

To invoke "states' rights" is to be suspect of wanting to deny "human rights" and similar charges of selfishness greet *any* attack on the tendency of government to grow, but more particularly when attention is called to failures by government in the field of human welfare.

Has the idea of a federation of sovereign states been proven unworkable because here and there selfish individuals used state government to impose on the freedom of some? Isn't there something to be said for a system wherein people can vote with their feet if government becomes too oppressive? Let a state pile on taxes beyond a bearable limit and business and industry start moving out and the people follow.

Let us think very carefully before switching to a system in which these states become administrative districts enforcing uniform laws and regulations.

No government could possibly muster a group capable of making the multitudinous decisions that must be made every day to keep a society like ours moving.

If a state is to be great it must call upon the greatness of the people. And the people must be prepared to give a portion of their time to public affairs because government is their business.

The only alternative to the people running government is government running the people.

18. THE MORALITY GAP AT BERKELEY

THERE has been a leadership gap and a morality and decency
gap at the University of California at Berkeley where a small
minority of beatniks, radicals and filthy speech advocates have
brought such shame to and such a loss of confidence in a great
University that applications for enrollment were down 21%
in 1967 and are expected to decline even further.

You have read about the report of the Senate Subcommittee
on Un-American Activities—its charges that the campus has
become a rallying point for Communists and a center of
sexual misconduct. Some incidents in this report are so bad,
so contrary to our standards of decent human behavior that
I cannot recite them to you in detail.

But there is clear evidence of the sort of things that should
not be permitted on a university campus.

The report tells us that many of those attending were
clearly of high-school age. The hall was entirely dark except
for the light from two movie screens. On these screens the
nude torsos of men and women were portrayed from time to
time in suggestive positions and movements.

Three rock and roll bands played simultaneously. The

(From a speech at the Cow Palace, May 12, 1966.)

smell of marijuana was thick throughout the hall. There were signs that some of those present had taken dope. There were indications of other happenings that cannot be mentioned here.

How could this happen on the campus of a great University? It happened because those responsible abdicated their responsibilities.

The dance was only called to a halt when janitors finally cut off the power in the gymnasium forcing those attending to leave.

And this certainly is not the only sign of a leadership gap on the campus.

It began when so-called "free-speech advocates," who in truth have no appreciation of freedom, were allowed to assault and humiliate an officer of the law. This was the moment when the ringleaders should have been taken by the scruff of the neck and thrown off of the campus—permanently.

It continued through the filthy speech movement, through activities of the Vietnam Day Committee and all this has been allowed to go on in the name of academic freedom.

What in Heaven's name does academic freedom have to do with rioting, with anarchy, with attempts to destroy the primary purpose of the University which is to educate our young people?

These charges must neither be swept under the rug by a timid administration or by public apologists for the University. The public has a right to know from open hearings whether the situation at Berkeley is as the report says.

The citizens who pay the taxes that support the University also have a right to know that, if the situation is as the report says, that those responsible will be fired, that the University will be cleaned up and restored to its position as a major institution of learning and research.

For this reason I today have called on the State Legislature to hold public hearings into the charges of Communism and blatant sexual misbehavior on the campus. I have sent personal wires to Senator Hugh Burns, the President Pro Tem of the Senate and to Assembly Speaker Jesse Unruh urging that they hold joint public hearings.

Only in this way can we get at the facts. Only this way can we find who is responsible for the degradation of a great University.

Only this way can we determine what steps must be taken to restore the University to its position, steps that might go even beyond what I have already suggested.

Yes, there are things that can be done at the University even if a hearing is never held. This administration could make changes. It could demand that the faculty jurisdictions be limited to academic matters.

It could demand that the administrators be told that it is their job to administer the University properly and if they don't we will find someone who will.

The faculty could also be given a code of conduct that would force them to serve as examples of good behavior and decency for the young people in their charge.

When those who advocate an open mind keep it open at both ends with no thought process in the middle, the open mind becomes a hose for any idea that comes along. If scholars are to be recognized as having a right to press their particular value judgments, perhaps the time has come also for institutions of higher learning to assert themselves as positive forces in the battles for men's minds.

This could mean they would insist upon mature, responsible conduct and respect for the individual from their faculty members and might even call on them to be proponents of those ethical and moral standards demanded by the great majority of our society.

These things could be done and should be done. The people not only have a right to know what is going on at their universities, they have a right to expect the best from those responsible for it.

19. TELEVISION AND POLITICS

FREE enterprisers in America still recognize and put up with the need for some regulation of business, industry and broadcasting by government.

But I suspect that most believe as I do, that regulation should be minimal and should not go beyond the amount necessary to insure that the rights of each of us, along with public health and safety, are protected.

There is a difference between regulation and control.

Free men recognize the need for some regulation by government.

But sometimes, well-intentioned men in government—even in a nation such as ours—in their efforts to insure equality and protect the rights of the people—cross over the borderline that separates regulation from control.

This has happened in many areas, at many echelons of government. The higher the echelon of government that regulates or controls, the more of us those regulations or controls affect.

(From a talk before the California Broadcasters Association, San Francisco.)

That, incidentally, is one reason I believe that government is best when, as much as possible, is kept at the echelon closest to the people.

As long as there is freedom of movement in this country, a man can walk away from onerous or unjust local regulations and even state regulations.

It is more difficult if controls are imposed at the national level.

All too often they have been.

We can all cite examples: the farmer who cannot grow what he wants without being subject to fines; the members of the religious sect fined and jailed without trial for failure to pay Social Security. In a nation where religion is recognized as a cause for exempting a man from bearing arms, these people had livestock and farm machinery seized for violation of a federal regulation.

The radio and TV industry, regulated of necessity because the airways belong to the people, has often been threatened with regulations and commission decisions that go beyond regulation and fall into the "government knows best" classification.

All of us recall Newton Minow and his description of television as a vast wasteland and the decision by certain FCC members to upgrade its quality.

Just recently, we had the FCC proposal that free time must be offered the opponents of cigarette smoking to compensate for the time tobacco companies buy.

Now, not to smoke is a laudable thing to do (I don't smoke), but the sale of tobacco and the smoking of tobacco are not illegal.

It makes one wonder whether the FCC is going to demand free time for the opponents of beer and ale, or the opponents of sports, or the opponents of religions.

Does Father indeed know best in these areas?

I understand the FCC would also have broadcasting companies divest themselves of sports enterprises and limit the number of commercials that can be shown during an event. Where indeed does regulation end and control begin?

I do believe there are some areas in which the FCC must rule, and I certainly have no objection to the equal time rule when it comes to politics.

In fact, I kind of like that idea.

Incidentally, I am not one of those who worries that television has upset our conduct of politics.

Those who scare us with stories that skilled performers can use the camera's magic to the end that all public offices will be filled with actors aren't really talking sense. In the first place, show business pays better. But in the second place, they reveal an ignorance of what the camera can actually do.

Television, even more than radio, is actually a return to our old-time tradition of taking to the stump. When our nation was sparsely settled it was possible for a candidate making the circuit to be seen by almost all the voters. As we grew in size and numbers, only a few actually saw the candidate. They made their decision on what they had heard or read about him.

But now, via the medium of television, they all can see him and hear him. And let me reveal something known to actors —you can't lie to the camera. When it rolls in for that bigger-than-life closeup, you'd better mean what you say, for insincerity will show up like a putty nose.

I think that television has made it possible for more people than ever before to judge a man on his merits. With whatever faults can be assessed against television, in this instance it is the hero. It has brought us back to the political stump meeting where the voters can look and listen and decide.

There is an area of political coverage, however, that has many people disturbed for which, I am almost sure, there will never be an entirely satisfactory answer.

That is the area of elections coverage, especially involving the use of computers and the quick forecasts of victory or defeat.

Nobody can be certain what the effect really is in California from national predictions in New York, which is three hours ahead of us.

In 1964, it was obvious that Lyndon Johnson had won long before California polls were closed. But it is not obvious what the net effect was in California.

Did Republicans quit going to the polls because the Presidency was lost and therefore hurt the chances of their statewide candidates? Or did Democrats, victory already in hand, not bother to vote and thus hurt their local candidates? Or did both?

We don't really know, but we are concerned that, even if Democrats and Republicans don't vote in equal numbers, advance victory disclosures breed voter apathy.

I do not know what the answer is, but I am inclined to go along with those who, in national elections would have polls opening and closing at the same time—not the same hour but the same time—throughout the nation.

Maybe some will think this is not practical and maybe there is a better answer. Regardless, this I believe is a problem that needs solving.

But generally speaking political reporting on both radio and television is good and improving.

And I think that as these media, like newspapers continue to develop specialists in the area of political reporting, it will improve even more.

Up to now I have pretty much been discussing commercial radio and television, but there is another facet of American television—educational television or public television.

And this is a little different matter from commercial television.

Certainly the broad concept is laudable. Non-profit television, supported by public subscriptions, foundations or philanthropies or by those for whom it provides services, such as school districts, can and does provide a useful function.

Educational or public television can be educational in

the very broad sense, presenting programs of importance and significance that have an intensive, if not extensive, viewership.

But I do not believe in federal subsidies for television, any more than I believe in them for any other form of communications—newspapers, magazines, radio.

And I believe even less in government-owned or operated public communications media, including television.

Yet there are hints of government-operated public television on the horizon. By public, I mean, as opposed to closed-circuit television—I mean television that any owner of a VHF or UHF television set can put up.

Now I know there is government-operated television in many nations including Britain—where it got so bad they had to let private enterprise come in and open a competing network.

And even in Britain, once the people were given a choice, it became clear that they preferred to choose their own programs instead of having their government choose them for them.

But pressure groups in this country continue to press for government-sponsored public television.

TV Guide recently noted that a committee of prominent people has been formed, sponsored by six foundations, "to drum up grass-roots excitement for non-commercial video's potentials."

The magazine adds: ". . . while lobbying for pending congressional legislation creating a federally-supported TV service is ruled out as one motive, it is hard to see how this could not be uppermost in the minds of committee leaders."

Looking around in our own state we recently discovered that the television advisory committee set up under the last administration has some pretty grandiose plans also.

Looking into these we found that the state has bought engineering surveys charting a state-wide television network —in fact two networks—with the announced goal of bringing "educational television to every community in California having a population of 1,000 or more."

In order to accomplish this goal, the advisory committee proposes an elaborate state-owned and operated interconnecting network, including microwave links, translators, community antenna television and even existing phone company facilities.

Under the plan the state could own and operate up to 12 new television stations; it would operate a video tape and film library, and a distribution system for delivery of tape and film to stations.

Now, what does all this mean to us?

It means, for one thing, the state goes into direct competition with private television.

Even more important, it has the dangerous potential of putting the state into the propaganda business.

The power to subsidize is the power to control and complete ownership gives complete control.

I am totally opposed to putting the state into the control, and dissemination directly to the public, of information.

No matter how well-intentioned an administration might be, I am convinced given that kind of power, no government could long deal honestly with the people concerning its activities.

20. THE DEMOCRATIC PARTY LEFT *US*

Most South Carolinians are, as I am, relatively new converts to Republicanism. We all started out as Democrats but somehow the Democratic party went away and left us.

It left us when it switched to so many philosophies and policies that we could not accept, the philosophy that big government is the best government, the philosophy that whoever the Democratic president may be, knows best.

It left us when it decided a few men in Washington know better than we do what is good for us and know better than we do how to spend our money.

State and local governments are buried now under a mass of 400 federal-aid appropriations, 170 separate federal-aid programs, administered by 21 federal departments and agencies, 150 Washington bureaus and 400 regional offices.

It is no wonder the Department of Housing and Urban Development is spending $30,000 on "A Study of the Means by which Local Governments Obtain Information on Federal Aid."

(From speeches in Columbia, South Carolina and Louisville, Kentucky.)

We have to spend money to find out how to give it away.

Of course some governments have not waited for federal aid in the area of finding out how to get federal aid. California, for example, has whole offices of people in Washington trying to get some of that federal money. There are offices there representing the state finance office, the legislature, the university, the state colleges and at least three cities and one water district.

And despite all this, you know, Californians still send more money to Washington than they get back.

We began in 1960 with a New Frontier and we progressed to a Great Society and during the process the civilian bureaucracy of the federal government has grown two-and-one-half times as fast as the increase in population. The payroll increased 7½ times and total government spending has increased 8½ times.

Somewhere a voice says, "But that is due to the Vietnam war." And it is true that defense spending since 1960 is up 68 percent—but non-defense spending is up 97 percent.

The deficits for these several years total $50 billion and the credibility gap is almost as big.

A year ago the President assured us he would stay within the budget and even cut it back by some $3 billion. After the election we learned that spending would be $14 billion over the budget. Then came the first prediction of the present year's budget deficit: $8½ billion. Now they admit to $11 billion but, just in case, they've asked for authority to accommodate a deficit of $29 billion.

I am part of government now (a funny thing happened to me on the way to Death Valley) but I am just as fearful as I ever was about government's capacity for growth and government's appetite for power.

I have observed first-hand government's resistance to change and the savage anger of some when any effort is made to reduce the size of its structure.

But I have learned also it can be reduced.

Fortunately, all of us in our administration in California were totally inexperienced; we had not learned all the things that cannot be done. For one thing, we set out to keep our campaign promises—and once the people got over their shock, they sort of took to the idea.

We had quite a tourist trade in California last year during our election. The Vice-President, practically all of the Cabnet, some well known in-laws, and a couple of Senators.

One of them, a young Senator from Massachusetts, came to warn the people of California against voting for someone totally inexperienced in public life. Now, if memory serves me correctly, that young Senator had never held office before he became a Senator. As a matter of fact, he'd never held a job.

Our "visitors" told us that the problems are too complex for simple answers, until gradually we have accepted government by mystery. The idea is that only a chosen elite in the nation's Capitol can make the decisions and find the answers.

Government is a mystery and it is certainly doing nothing to make it simpler. There seems to have evolved a special kind of government language, incomprehensible to simple citizens like ourselves.

For example, what does a city councilman or a county commissioner, or even a governor do when he receives a report from the Department of Housing and Urban Development, that reads, "Action oriented orchestration of innovation inputs, generated by escalation of meaningful indigenous decision making dialogue, focusing on multi-linked problem complexes, can maximize the vital thrust toward a non-alienated and viable, urban infra-structure."

I know no Republican gathering could be held here unless it contained a great many former Democrats and perhaps many who are still affiliated with that party. I know you are present because you, too, are deeply disturbed over the course our country has been following during these recent years. I know, too, the feeling of guilt or betrayal that some of you feel particularly those who have changed party registration. I know because I too, felt that wrench and was surprised to discover how deeply ingrained is the sense of party loyalty.

When the leadership of that party repudiated the constitutional concepts of individual freedom, local autonomy and states' rights; when it embraced the 19th-century philosophy of rule of the many by the few; that one man in the White House was omnipotent, and that a little intellectual elite in the nation's Capitol can engage in social tinkering even to the extent of telling working men and women of this nation how and with whom they must share the fruit of their labor, then I say the leadership of that party betrayed us.

Today the leadership of the honorable party of Jefferson and Jackson has abandoned the dream of individual freedom, has lost its faith in the people's ability to determine their own destiny, believes only in centralized government and an all-powerful state. We find it is the Republican Party that is polarized around a belief in constitutional limits on the power of government, belief in the right of the individual to freedom of choice, a belief in a federal system of sovereign states and not just administrative districts of a central government.

Thousands upon thousands of Americans, those forgotten men and women who work and support the communities and pay for all the social experimenting are groping for answers to their doubts, seeking a cause in which they can invest their idealism and their energy. They are too self-reliant to sell their dreams of the future for the dull security of the antique.

They believe in this nation as a nation under God, and that our national purpose is to provide the ultimate in individual freedom consistent with law and order. That their freedom is theirs by divine right and not by government whim. They love peace, but not at any price. They believe that a cause worth dying for is a cause worth winning.

21. THE ROLE OF STATE LEGISLATORS

EVERYWHERE we see the voters approving measures to improve the pay and the working conditions of their legislators.

I am proud to say that much of the leadership in upgrading the legislatures has come from California where men in both parties have worked diligently to improve the quality of those who serve and incentives for those capable of serving.

Just a year ago California voters approved setting legislators' salaries at $16,000 a year plus at $25 a day expenses when the legislature is in session. In California, it hardly pays to run for Congress any more—especially if you have a governor who will call you into special session now and then. So far, though, there has been no indication that a California governor can count on extra votes as a display of gratitude for issuing such calls.

Of course, no governor has a right to expect any legislator to vote his way as a favor or because of political expediency.

(From a speech before the National Conference of State Legislative Leaders, San Francisco.)

But it goes without saying he does have a right to expect every legislator to vote the way he thinks is best for his state, irrespective of political considerations. By the same token, the legislature has a right to expect its efforts to be received and signed on that basis and no other.

In these complex times, the legislature is no place for the prima donna or for the legislator who worries more about protocol and prerogatives than he does about his duties to his state and his constitutency.

In the early days of my administration we had our problems, not only with the members of the other party, but also with the members of our own.

In retrospect, I think this is understandable.

We were the new boys in town. There was much to be done and much to be learned.

So we learned by doing. Some people described the early days of my administration as a honeymoon. My reply was that if it was a honeymoon, I was sleeping alone. And then, looking around at some of those who allegedly were on the honeymoon with me, I decided that sleeping alone was not such a bad idea.

Well, that is the case for two legislative houses. There is, of course, the third house and here, too, the old stereotyped image is fading. The picture of shadowy figures offering favors in an atmosphere of bacchanalian revelry is being replaced by recognized and registered lobbyists representing everything from higher education to business associations and industries. Certainly no one denies the right of the individual or group to such representation. But here, too, you and I have a responsibility to consult now and then directly with the principals to make sure they have been correctly informed regarding proposed legislation and executive actions so that a lobbyist is truly representing their viewpoint and not just promoting his own political bias.

My feeling is that the day of the old-time wheeler-dealer is going. The day when such men could control votes with campaign contributions, parties, girls and booze is about over.

Speaker Unruh has been quoted as saying that "if a man can be bought with a lunch, he doesn't belong in Sacramento."

He is right. But if a man can be bought for any price, he does not belong in Sacramento or in any state capitol. This is no indictment of the average lobbyist, who has a tough job and does it well. We look on many as friends and some as advisors.

But we also from time to time meet in my office with their bosses. We do not mean to eliminate the middleman. We want them to know firsthand what we are doing and why we are doing it and we do not want anything lost in the translation.

My administration makes no bones about being business-oriented. A healthy business climate means a healthy economy and a healthy economy benefits all our people in jobs, in added tax revenues for added government services, in many other ways.

In addition, we believed and we are finding out it is true, that a government operated on business-like principles is a more efficient, more economical government.

Our entire system is based on a network of checks and balances. And among the most important of those is the two-party system where one party checks the other as soon as it gets out of balance.

There are those who complain that our system is slow, and unwieldy, and more designed for an 18th-century rural society than for the technological society of the 20th century.

I do not believe that.

The faster science and technology progress, the more necessary it is for our political scientists and those in government to stand back and take a good hard look at where we are going, and how fast.

Science and technology are servants. They can become our masters, if in our hurry to keep up with them, we lose sight of what government is all about.

The legislative and the executive, regardless of party, must work together in some degree of harmony if the states are to progress and if they are to maintain their sovereignty and not become mere administrative districts of an all-powerful federal government. And this is probably the most pressing problem we face and it puts us in the forward combat position in the defense of freedom. Those who sneeringly reject the term "states' rights" ignore the great part the state plays in providing a built-in guaranty against tyranny.

But to retain our rights at the state and local levels, we must also accept our responsibilities at those levels.

If we fail in that task, if we do not meet the responsibilities we are called on to meet, the people will turn, however reluctantly, to the federal government for solutions to all their problems.

And the federal government will eagerly and willingly accept that responsibility.

This, then, is the challenge of our times, to the states and to those who legislate in them, and to those who administer the laws—to meet the responsibilities our times demand of us.

And to do it in such a way that our states can not only survive, but also maintain their sovereignty, their integrity and the hope they offer to future generations.

Our government was meant to be run by the people and the people can do this only if government and the control of the people's affairs is kept close at hand. In the most unique social order ever conceived by man, our own, we in state government occupy what could be an almost unique position. We must have the wisdom and the will not to take unto ourselves powers and rights that are better left to the individual and local communities, and at the same time we must prevent a higher echelon of government from weakening our ability and determination to fulfill this function.